aunt joan's caBin
. . . a year's journey to joy

DEE PRESS

First Printing, 2025

ISBN: 979-8-9942142-0-6

Dee Press LLC

501 Union St

STE 545 PMB 307719

Nashville, TN. 37219

www.DeePress.net

dedication . . .

For all my trans sisters and brothers past, present and future.

For the cisgender people that love(d) and support(ed) them on their journey.

contents . . .

prologue . . .

January 5, 2024

I was in TJ Maxx this morning, looking at their clearance jewelry.

A middle-aged woman with silver glasses stepped uncomfortably close to me. She reached aggressively in front of me to grab a box that contained a pair of Mickey Mouse earrings. She looked at them briefly and tossed them back.

She said, with an annoyed voice, "Why does everything have to be Mickey Mouse?!"

I replied in my sweetest voice, "You don't like Mickey?"

"No, I don't!" she said sharply.

"You don't hear that too often," I said, repressing the urge to say, "Then why did you pick them up?"

"I'll tell you somethin' else, I REALLY don't like that Disney World! It's nothin' but a bunch of FREAKS down there!"

Still trying to stay sweet, I said, "Really? You might want to be careful, because you never know when you might run into a 'freak.'"

"That's the truth!" she huffed. "But I tell you, when I do, I just say, 'May the Lord forgive ya!'"

Dropping my sweetness and employing my deepest "man voice," I bellowed, "And may the Lord forgive you."

Her eyes got big, she looked like she'd seen a ghost. She hurried off.

"I hope you have a nice day!"

She didn't look back at me.

I've wondered if she has shared this story too.

introduction . . .

I am a trans person.

I started gender-affirming hormone therapy (GAHT) in March of 2023.

I made no "official" announcement, only sharing my decision with close friends. Although social (public) transition was my goal, I decided I would take a stepped approach to it. Over the next several months, my wardrobe and appearance shifted to a more nondescript androgynous look. The only exception was when I visited friends in Florida, where I dressed fully feminine.

The changes that occurred during my first year on GAHT (or HRT) were amazing. I never doubted or regretted my decision.

By late fall of 2023, I was determined that I was going to begin my social transition. For me, social transition would involve presenting fully as feminine, using feminine pronouns, and a legal name change.

My social media presence has always been very limited. I have a very short list of curated "friends" compared to most people. If something I post online gets twenty "likes," I consider it an enormous success. Over a couple of years, I had posted several pictures of myself presenting as feminine that had gotten some positive reactions.

On January 5, 2024, I posted the TJ Maxx story about my experience being out in the wild as a girl. It made no reference to my being trans.

On January 30, 2024, I made my first public declaration that I am a trans person and that I would be seeking a legal name change. I received great support from my friends online.

I quickly realized, by the questions and reactions I got from people, that there was very little known about the trans experience. Many people expressed concern for me based on the idea that living as my authentic self would be trying and unpleasant.

I don't know that it was a conscious decision, but I began sharing journal entries with stories and anecdotes from my daily life as I began my public/social transition.

The following pages contain a selection of snippets from my life in my second year of transition. Interactions, experiences, "firsts," and some looking back on my past through the eyes of my now-authentic self are included. I think the most surprising thing about these entries is just how "ordinary" they are. I am not special. I, like most trans people, just want to live my life like everyone else.

Every trans person has their own individual journey. One of the biggest obstacles to widespread understanding of people who identify as trans is that no two stories are identical. There is no "How to Trans" guidebook. My journey is my story alone. My opinions, decisions, feelings, comments, etc., are mine and mine alone.

The best thing about my transition is the great joy I now feel in my life. I sincerely hope that you can feel that joy in these words.

As the following are journal entries, the original format and structure has been retained. For the sake of privacy, names have been changed or omitted.

Thank you for reading this.

You are very kind.

I am very lucky.

a rose by any other name . . .

January 30, 2024

This won't come as a surprise to most of you who have seen and commented on my recently posted profile pics and tales from TJ Maxx: I am a trans person.

I am approaching my one-year anniversary of HRT (Hormone Replacement Therapy).

I won't bore you with details of my journey, but those closest to me already know what an amazing positive difference it has made in my life, both mentally and physically.

Although I haven't felt the need to post much about my transition, please know I am fine if you have any questions.

I am writing this today because I am preparing to petition the court to legally change my name. In some ways, this has felt like the biggest challenge I have faced thus far. Many of us trans and non-binary folks can't wait to get rid of our birth names. Some choose to refer to their former monikers as their "dead name." Always remember that everyone's journey is different, and I have nothing but respect for any individual's feelings on the subject.

I would like you to know that I don't dislike "Stephen." I do not consider "him" in any way to be "dead." The fact is, "Stephen" has been very good to me over the years. "He" has been my provider and my protector. "He" is relatively smart, talented, nice (most of the time), and hilarious . . . and modest.

On March 27, 2023, I finally allowed myself to show "him" that I love "her" by beginning this journey. So far, everything about my transition has been a positive gain for me. My overly sentimental attachment to a name had, for the first time, made me feel that I needed to give something up to achieve the next gain.

I have accepted that "Stephen" is just a name and nothing more. I am retiring "Stephen" and know that the things that made "him" are very much "alive."

I am me.

Admittedly, it has been fun and sometimes a little silly deciding what my new name would be. One friend advocated for "Serena." She was thinking about the strength and beauty of Serena Williams, while I was doe-eyed for the kookiness, creativity, and groovy short skirts of "Cousin Serena" from *Bewitched*. I didn't think I could live up to either one. I was afraid and stressed about picking the wrong name.

Ultimately, I decided on a name that someone else picked for me.

My parents decided to have a third child (me) for one reason: my mother wanted a "girl." Mom was convinced, during her entire difficult pregnancy, that I was going to be a "girl" (okay . . . I know, right?!).

After I started HRT last spring and before Mom got sick, I was able to have a conversation with her about what my name would have been had I been the "girl" she wanted. I honestly expected it to be dreadful because her mother's name was Alberta!

It wasn't dreadful. I genuinely loved it and have decided to take it as my name. It feels right to me.

It will likely be a couple of months before it is legal, but I wanted to share with you that my petition will be that STEPHEN EUGENE HAYNES will now be known as DEANNA JEAN HAYNES.

Feel free to call me Dee.

Contrary to Mr. Shakespeare's quote, with HRT, I smell a lot sweeter these days!

it matters . . .

February 1, 2024

I have a student in one of my classes who presents as feminine.

During a class discussion this morning, they shared something. I referenced their statement when talking to another student.

My reference began with, "She said . . ." I immediately realized that I had no idea what their pronoun preference was.

At the end of class, I asked to speak to the student. I apologized to them for my assumption and asked if they had a preference. They said they didn't and that they didn't let it bother them if someone addressed them as "ma'am" or "sir."

I shared that we had that in common and that I, too, got both "ma'am" and "sir."

The student smiled and turned to leave.

They turned back and said, "I've been wanting to tell you something."

I said, "Sure."

They said, "I want you to know that on the first day of class I was so scared and nervous. Then you walked in. The first thing I noticed was your beautiful fingernails. It was amazing. I was so happy and relieved. Thank you for that."

I smiled broadly and said, "You don't need to thank me, but that makes me very happy. Please know if you ever need anything, just talk to me."

I managed to make it back to my office before I cried.

March 3, 2024

I often get asked what the student reaction has been to me.

Regarding "you be you," most of this generation really appears not to put much thought into it. My students are always respectful to me and their peers in the classroom. I even occasionally get comments about my nail polish, my "cute" fuzzy Snoopy sweatshirt, or my jewelry.

I only have one student who has made it obvious he doesn't approve of me, but even he has never in any way been disrespectful. I find it highly amusing that he tries very hard not to laugh at my corny jokes or comments in class.

As I've said before, I have never felt compelled to make some big announcement that I am this or that. Even if I did feel that was the route I wanted to go, it would not be appropriate to stand in front of a class and share such a personal aspect of my life. My approach has been to gradually make changes in my work appearance as the semester progressed. Students are smart and can figure things out.

There was one exception.

There is a student that I haven't had in class in a while and won't ever again. Although he no longer has a need for any of my courses, he has continued to seek my counsel and advice throughout his academic career.

I consider having a student want to discuss things with me the highest honor and responsibility.

I don't know when or how often I'll have an interaction with this student, as it could be multiple times a week or it might be weeks between talks. He comes from a very conservative family, though I've never had any indication that he might have a problem with someone like me.

I felt strongly that I needed to let him know what was going on with me so that he wouldn't be upset or confused if he heard any comments about it from his peers.

We met a couple of months ago to talk about what he wanted to accomplish this semester. I also wanted to encourage him to start moving on, lining something up for the summer. We talked about those things, and finally I told him I wanted to tell him something about myself. I let him know that after he heard this, I would understand if he needed to step away from talking to me. I also said that if that happened, it didn't mean he couldn't contact me in the future if he needed anything.

I looked down before I spoke because I didn't want to misread any initial expression on his face. I told him I was trans. I then shared that my appearance was going to become decidedly feminine over the semester.

There was a pause.

When I looked up, I saw a huge smile on his face.

He said, "I am so proud of you. Are you kidding? This changes nothing. I am so proud and happy for you."

With great relief, I said, "Thank you." We continued our conversation about his semester.

As our talk progressed, I turned away to look something up for him.

When I turned back, I saw this mischievous grin on his face. I said, "Ok, what are you thinking?"

He said, "Nothing."

"I know better than that, spill it."

He said, "I was just thinking about those times you told us to think of you as our creepy uncle."

You reach that age as a teacher when students will say to you, "You remind me of my dad," or "You sound like my mom." It's devastating the first couple of times you hear it, but you learn to appreciate it. I had taken to saying, "Don't think of me as your mom (or dad); just think of me as your creepy uncle."

Anyway . . .

He said, "I was just thinking about those times you told us to think of you as our creepy uncle. I never said this to you because I was afraid it would hurt your feelings, but every time you said that I always thought, 'You're not like a creepy uncle; you're more like a cool aunt.' And now I get to think of you as my cool aunt."

. . . I know, right?

It was as precious as it sounds.

I am very lucky.

March 4, 2024

I legally have a new name. My name is Deanna Jean Haynes.

As I was typing this recap of my name change day, I was struck with the thought, "Who cares?" I went to the courthouse, the Social Security office, and the DMV. Hardly the makings of a lengthy essay. To most people, this would just be a boring day of life's errands.

I don't think I am special. I don't think my experiences are any more important than anyone else's. But I really dreaded today. No one should have to dread such a wonderful thing happening for them—I LOVE my name. I resent the fact that I had to "out" myself to take care of what should be a regular, joyous task.

Are people going to be rude to me?

Hate me just because of who I am?

Refuse to change my name?

Considering the current political climate and the stories we've all heard, all of those were real possibilities. I refuse to be afraid. I do not wish to invite confrontation. It shouldn't feel like this for anyone.

I don't like feeling or sounding like I am surprised when someone is nice to me or treats me with respect.

Adventures in changing a name . . .

Some friends had suggested that I dress in a more low-key manner so as not to stand out and look like I was trying too hard. I had decided to wear my black "funeral dress," but when I got up this morning, I said to myself, "No way, this isn't a funeral day." It was very warm today, and the first day of our spring break, so I chose a green vintage-style dress. I don't think I necessarily stood out, but I was the only person in the courtroom today who wore a dress.

The officer who checked me at security was very kind. I wouldn't say he flirted, but he did talk to me a lot more than he did to the men ahead of me. He also took some time to "mansplain" why women's shoes often set off the metal detector. Karmically, I'm sure I'm due some mansplaining sessions, so I didn't mind. I just said, "Oh, really?" a couple of times. He held the door open for me to enter the courtroom.

It's a small courtroom that was full by 9 a.m.

I had been told by a friend that this judge was inclusive. When she entered the courtroom, I immediately noticed her blue eyeshadow—blue eyeshadow all the way up to the eyebrows. This was going to be okay.

There were several estate/probate cases that didn't take long. Then three divorce cases—so cringy and uncomfortable to sit through. I wasn't the only person to have their business broadcast for everyone in the room. All the cases moved very quickly.

The judge then announced she would handle some name change cases.

I was called up.

When I got up to stand before the judge, I noticed the officer who had talked to me while going through security standing in the back of the courtroom. I wondered if he'd regret having been nice to me.

I was sworn in, and the judge asked me if I was "Stephen Eugene Haynes."

"Yes, Ma'am."

"And you wish to change your name to Deanna Jean Haynes?"

"Yes, Ma'am."

She then said, "So you are keeping your last name?"

"Yes, Ma'am."

"I'm glad."

I can only guess why she said that.

She then said, "I have to ask you some questions now, and I'd like you to know that if it were my choice, I would have no interest in asking them, but I am required to do so."

"Yes, Ma'am, I understand."

I had already looked it up and knew what she'd ask me. Primarily, they dealt with making sure I wasn't avoiding debts by changing my name. I answered the questions.

She banged her gavel, smiled, and said, "Congratulations."

I cannot begin to explain the immediate weight I felt lifted from me in that moment. I wasn't expecting that at all and thought it would dissipate quickly. It hasn't yet.

I was off to pick up the official order.

As I left the courtroom, that same security officer held the door open for me again. He smiled and said, "I really hope you have a nice day."

I walked down to the office to get my paperwork. Some lawyers from the previous cases were finishing up, so I had to wait a minute.

While waiting, a woman I had noticed in the courtroom came into the office. She patted me on the back and said, "Congratulations!"

I said, "Thank you."

She said, "We're name change buddies and both starting new chapters!" She shared that she was sixty-seven years old and had been divorced for five years. She was finally changing back to her maiden name. She added that she was tired of that "albatross hanging around my neck."

One of the ladies in the office was free and asked Albatross Lady if she could help her. She patted me on the back again and said, "No! This gal is next."

To my knowledge, that is the first time I've been called "gal." Yes, I liked it . . .

Next up was the Social Security office.

Since court had gone so smoothly, I was confident there might be a bump or two here. Albatross Lady showed up about ten minutes after me, and we got to chat a bit. I was called back, and everyone was nice and professional.

No bumps.

Next was the DMV . . . ugh.

The TN DMV is never pleasant for anyone. I've heard stories from friends about how rudely they'd been treated by some DMV employees. I felt certain that, because I had such a good experience so far, I was due for some rudeness.

I walked in, and the place was packed. Again, I was the only person wearing a dress—I did stand out here. I checked in with a woman who was very kind and helpful. It was going to be a long wait.

As I made my way across the crowded waiting room, a teenage girl said, "I love your dress."

A big smile and, "Thank you."

There were no empty seats available, and several men were standing against the walls. I found a spot along a wall and was ready to settle in against it.

Then a sweet "ice cream" moment.

"Ma'am, ma'am, take my seat." A handsome man was standing and motioning me over to his seat.

"Thank you so much, you're very kind, but I don't mind standing. I don't want to take your seat, sir."

"Really, ma'am, I insist."

He leaned against the wall, and I took his seat.

I call these moments "ice cream" because, just like eating ice cream, when they happen, I have feelings of guilt—but damn, do they taste good.

I won't complain about the wait. I was eventually called back. The woman who helped me was pleasant.

Then the moment I had dreaded arrived.

"I need to see your current driver's license."

As I handed it to her, I said, "I don't really look like this anymore."

She took the old license, looked at it for a minute, and finally looked up at me with a sweet smile on her face and said, "No, ma'am, you sure don't."

That "ma'am" and the several that followed in our conversation were very kind and respectful.

I hope the day comes when no one will have to worry about whether they will be respected or not.

I am very grateful for all the lovely people who made this a great day for me.

It was really an amazing day.

I am very lucky.

reflections . . .

March 24, 2024

This weekend will see Easter Sunday, the Trans Day of Visibility, and my one-year anniversary of HRT.

It makes me smile that all three will be this weekend.

As with any milestone, I've been thinking a lot about the past year. Obviously, it has been a mixed year—the amazing peace and joy I have found in being able to be my authentic self, and the challenge of losing my mom and dad.

I have had several people ask and/or assume that I had waited to start my transition until after my parents passed. I started my HRT prior to mom getting so sick; dad had been in and out of the nursing home for almost two years at that point.

Although I had started HRT before their passing, I made the decision not to tell them.

Growing up, my dad and I had little in common—a good relationship but never as close as he was to my two brothers. During my childhood, we didn't do a lot of things together that were just the two of us. He would take me to the circus every year when it came to town—set up in a shopping center parking lot. I loved it. When I was a teenager, we both enjoyed wrestling. I'm confident we found pleasure in it for very different reasons. We would watch the WWF (now WWE) on TV and sometimes go to local matches together.

The fact that Dad was very liberal surprised many people because he was a true "country boy." All his friends fell on the other side of the political spectrum. Politics was what really connected my dad and me in my adulthood. He truly believed that if "you're not hurtin' nobody, what you do is nobody's business."

By the time I made the decision to start HRT, Dad had already started to show signs of forgetting and mixing things up. I don't doubt he would have been supportive of me. I felt that telling him or showing up in a skirt at that point would lead to more confusion for him.

My mother and I always had a strained relationship.

Mom had a horrible childhood. She lost her dad very early, and her mother, to put it mildly, was a very disturbed soul. My mother was a good person and did a lot of nice things for many people in her life, but she carried demons from her past with her.

My relationship with my mother was very different from the one my brothers had with her. I never understood why until my therapist suggested a book to me. The title of the book took me aback a bit—not that I was offended by it, but I just didn't think it was possible that it was the reason my relationship with her was so much more challenging. The book was *WILL I EVER BE GOOD ENOUGH? Healing the Daughters of Narcissistic Mothers* by Dr. Karyl McBride.

OMG!

The book blew me away. So many of the cases cited in the book could have been written by me. Dr. McBride even points out the differences in how sons are treated differently in this family unit, and it matched my brothers' relationship with our mother.

The book was very affirming, but it also raised questions. Had I acted more feminine/daughterly in my childhood than I thought I had? Did my mother instinctively know about me all along? I suspect, on some level, the answer is "yes" to both questions.

Mom was not as liberal as Dad. I'd describe her as more passive when it came to politics. Even so, I had planned on telling her about my transition. I already knew what her reaction would be to the news. It was the same reaction I always got from her on any serious topic: "Well, whatever, you're going to do whatever you want to do anyway."

My real hesitation in telling her was that I knew at some point, some moment, she would be cruel about it. It would be used to hurt me at an opportune moment. My appearance, my weight, my vocation, my foster parenting, my dating men, my education, etc., were regularly turned into daggers when they could do the most harm.

There were a couple of moments I came close to having the conversation with her.

She noticed my nails were painted at dinner one night. I had been using clear polish for several years but had switched to color. She asked me why they were painted. I said, "I think it's pretty; I think it's pretty, I replied." The *Cabaret*/Sally Bowles quote was lost on her, and she quickly changed the subject before I could say anything else.

I had also planned to tell her when I asked what my name would have been if I had been born a girl. She was so happy telling me about "Deanna" that I decided not to change her mood.

She soon started severely hallucinating and began her rapid decline. She quickly was no longer in a state of mind that could comprehend the news.

When she entered the nursing home, something happened to me that had never happened before in my life. It seems so silly that it was a shock to me.

I was not presenting feminine at this time, but I had adopted a more androgynous look. A nurse stopped me in the hallway and said, "My God, you look just like your mother!"

I was speechless.

My entire life I had always been told I looked like my father. Since that day in the nursing home, I have only been told that I look like my mother.

one year . . .

March 30, 2024

Today is the day—one year since I placed the first estrogen patch on my body.

I know in the last few months I have gone from not talking about my transition publicly to posting regular harangues about it. I appreciate those of you who have made kind comments to me.

I thought, in recognition of my anniversary, I would share some of the random things I've learned or had affirmed in the past year:

- There is no "How to Trans" manual. There is no checklist. Everyone's journey is different.

- When you're trans and start your journey, you go from being dysphoric to euphoric. It is as amazing as it sounds.

- I have great joy.

- My therapist told me transitioning would be the "hardest thing you ever do." In all honesty, so far, it has been the easiest thing I have done.

- No one does this for fun.

- HRT basically puts you through a second puberty... yep.

- There are medical risks involved in transition.

-Many trans people lose family, friends, home, job, etc., to be themselves. I know how fortunate I am not to have had to face those challenges.

- Every time I need to use the restroom in a public setting, I feel a little stressed thinking that someone might make a scene.

- On this journey, I get to drag along some of the privileges I've enjoyed most of my life. Many of my trans brothers and sisters don't have that same experience. We really have no idea what someone else has lived or is living. Always show grace.

- I've had many more positive experiences dealing with people in public situations than negative ones.

- It's not every trans person's goal to pass.

- I pass better than I ever thought possible. I now realize it's not the most important thing to me.

- Some men lack any subtlety when they look at your chest.

- Having someone hold the door open for you is a lovely thing.

- A cute UPS guy giving you a wink can make your day.

- I learn new things about myself every day.

- Little nice surprises happen all the time.

- I have several amazing cis female friends who have been supportive and affirming from day one. There are still moments in conversations with them where my initial thought is, "Yikes," followed immediately by, "Oh, we can talk about that now." Then I smile.

- If I had grown up a female child, I would have been a very "girly" girl... and likely a bit of a slut in high school... and college... I know, right?

- I feel very fortunate to be a trans person.

- I think it's an amazing thing that I know things about men that women will never know, and I know things about women that men will never know. How cool is that?

- I am very lucky.

questions . . .

April 28, 2024

The most repeated reaction I've gotten from people who have felt comfortable talking to me about my transition has been a simple: "I don't get it..." I haven't experienced this being stated in a negative way, rather just as a sincere statement.

My reaction is always: "That's good! You shouldn't get it."

There is no way to truly explain or understand the experience of gender dysphoria. I'm not sure anyone who has everything in alignment—a cis person—could understand what it feels like not to have that feeling. I would much prefer someone to honestly say, "I don't get it," rather than assume that, as human beings, we are all easily defined by our genitalia. Trust me, there is plenty about it that I don't "get" either. There is also much I don't get about other folks. We are just the way we are.

"What are your pronouns?" ... or "What the heck are you?"

This is a topic that everyone has an opinion on, as pronouns have been weaponized in today's political environment. Please know my opinions on this topic are mine alone—I only speak for myself and have nothing but respect for those who feel differently.

When I started my transition, I labeled myself "trans-feminine."

"Wait, what does that mean? I thought you were a 'trans woman.'"

I chose "trans-feminine" because I wasn't sure how I felt about the word "woman." Growing up, I went through a male puberty, and I've navigated most of my life presenting as a male. I do know how I feel and how I feel most comfortable presenting. Those feelings and presentations are most aligned with the female gender—woman.

I sincerely have no way of knowing if who I am and what I feel makes me a "woman." I have not, nor will I ever, experience all the things a cis woman has experienced. I just know how I feel; maybe that's how a woman feels, or maybe it's different.

I don't know the answer.

I don't have to know the answer.

What I do know is that I feel feminine, so that's why I choose to identify as trans-feminine. I would like to stress that I only speak for myself and not anyone who identifies otherwise.

I am not offended in the least if someone calls me a trans woman or, when a friend says, "Now that you're a woman." Because the term "trans-feminine" is not well known, I usually just say that I am a "trans person." I want to be seen and treated as a person, and I honestly believe the rest is obvious without my having to say anything further.

My pronoun preference is she/her. I choose those because she/her most closely matches my presentation and feelings.

I made up my mind early in my journey that I would never let words, labels, or names hurt me. It truly doesn't matter what someone calls me if it is done with basic human respect. I haven't yet experienced someone intentionally using the wrong pronoun for me. I know that day will come, as it seems to be a rite of passage for trans folk today.

"When did you know?"

I've known as long as I can remember.

Most trans folks in my age range who "always knew" will tell you: "I knew, but I didn't know." I always knew I was different. I always knew I didn't fit in the "cis" world.

Looking back on my childhood, there were plenty of signs and dysphoric moments. The truth is I didn't know the words that described what I felt or that anyone else had those feelings. As a teenager, I thought I was "gay," as I was a "male" attracted to men. *(Note: Please don't assume that a trans-feminine person is attracted to men, or that a trans-masculine person is attracted to women.)* I adopted "gay" as my label for a long time, but honestly, I knew I really didn't fit into that world either.

I never had that big dramatic moment or feeling that you used to see in movies and television where I declared, "I am a woman trapped in a man's body!" I've never met a trans person who has used that phrase to describe their experience.

I'm not sure at what age I was able to put words to it. As I grew older, I would go through periods where I'd have makeup and a few nice outfits to wear in private but then decide that "phase" was over and throw it all out—rinse and repeat. A never-ending cycle.

"Why did you wait? Why now?"

I had decided many years ago that I would live as I wanted when I retired. This is a common feeling among trans people in my generation *(note: Not all trans people feel the need to transition at all)*. I was convinced that I could never pass as feminine enough to live a "normal life." I thought it would be a lot less trouble to transition when I didn't have to worry so much about social acceptance.

Then the pandemic happened.

I started asking myself: "Could I pass?" and "Does it matter?"

If it didn't really matter, why was I waiting? Wouldn't it be amazing to just be myself and not wait until I was an old lady to transition? ...okay, older lady... okay, maybe not lady... I seriously started to consider the implications if I went ahead and started the journey. I went back and forth, changing my mind almost daily for several months.

Then the political BS kicked into high gear—the TN legislature couldn't do enough to prove how anti-LGBTQ+ they could be. I knew the fear this placed in people like me—after all, that is the point.

Specifically, I thought about young people who were already scared and unsure of the feelings they were having. I was determined that fear would not be a reason to put off living authentically.

The rest, as they say, is HERstory—hah, see what I did there?

"How have students/colleagues reacted?"

I haven't felt any negativity from anyone.

Colleagues in my area have been very supportive. A few folks outside my area avoid looking at me; they might have always avoided looking at me, and I just notice it now. A couple of male colleagues have held doors open for me, which is always nice. The folks in HR were very kind and acted promptly with my name change. One thing they did surprised me. I had planned on requesting IT change my name/email at the end of the semester, to avoid confusing any of my current students. HR put in the request immediately—it made me happy that they were on top of it. It very much seems like it's not a big deal, which is the way it should be.

My students are not the sharpest knives in the drawer, but they are by far the nicest students I have ever worked with in my career. I've said before that I didn't feel the need to stand in front of my classes and declare that I am "this" or "that." I also haven't announced that I have a new name. They have seen my new name on emails, and my presentation is fully feminine at this point. There are a few students who didn't know what to make of me at first but now seem comfortable. I have not shared my preferred pronouns, so a few students still address me as "sir." It is always respectful. I've noticed most students now use "professor" instead of "sir," which is nice.

Most of my students this semester are male jocks. One class feels a bit like walking into a locker room. I was apprehensive about how it would go. It has turned out to be the class I look forward to the most this semester. I try hard to make my classroom an open space where students can freely talk and communicate respectfully. They have bought into that, making it a fun class.

They have taught me as much, if not more, than I've taught them.

"Are you going to have...?"

Yes, there is THE question I have been asked. I think it warrants its own entry, so I will talk about THAT at a later date.

fishy . . .

May 1, 2024

The University has a (very successful) fishing team. I refer to these students in my head as "fish guys."

Some professors don't enjoy having "fish guys" in class because they are gone to tournaments so often—they're in a constant state of catch...up (HA!) —that they're always playing catch-up. I like having "fish guys" in class. They are smart, funny, quintessential "good old boys," and decent speakers who tell great stories.

Yesterday in class, I heard a "fish guy" talking about a professor he doesn't like. If I hear a student talking negatively about another professor, I will usually point out that the problem is often that the student has or hasn't done something the professor wanted, or it's just a personality clash. In either case, the student needs to do their job: pass the class and move on with life.

Part of the conversation made me very happy.

Trying to smooth over his attitude toward the professor, I said, "Now come on, I've heard nothing but good things about his class, and I know he's a really nice guy."

Not giving in, he said, "Well, he hates me. I don't know why. But I tell you, he is so weird. He is the weirdest person I've ever met."

I smiled and proudly said, "Well, you just made my day."

"Why's that?"

Speaking as if I'd won a prize, I said, "You just stood in front of me and said he is the weirdest person you've ever met."

He looked straight at me, then down at my feet, then back to my face, and said, "...I might've spoken too soon."

Laughter all around.

I love these students.

TRANSportation . . .

May 5, 2024

I bought a new car yesterday.

It was a good experience, other than the spending money thing. I suppose at some point I won't feel the urge to share the trans moments I encounter daily, but honestly it is all still very new to me. I like sharing the positivity I experience.

So here goes:

There is always a little apprehension when entering male-dominated spaces. I always unfairly imagine male car salesmen as Neverland frat boys. I had already shopped online and knew the vehicles I was interested in seeing.

When I got out of my car, I just walked to them to check them out.

In no time at all I heard, "Good afternoon!"

I turned to face a salesman, and there it was... the stare. I think I'll talk about "the stare" in more detail in a later entry, but it's a look I get from both men and women, where they look at me and hold the gaze just a bit too long. It is always long enough that it feels awkward. Obviously, I have no idea what they are thinking, but I have a couple of theories.

I returned the greeting, and "the stare" was broken.

The salesman was very nice and helpful. After a few comparisons and a test drive, we went inside to his desk to talk numbers. Other than "the stare," there was nothing unusual or awkward about the encounter.

At a point, the sales manager joined us, and we reached a stalemate, where they weren't budging to get to my number. I got to do one of my favorite things: get up, say, "Thank you for your time, gentlemen," and walk out. I really wish I had brought my purse in, as picking it up and walking out is a great dramatic touch in such moments—it makes me feel very Alexis Carrington (if you get that reference, I love you and you're old).

I left and went for a late lunch with the hope I'd get a phone call asking me to come back.

I got the call and returned.

Happily, they had "run the numbers," and though they "weren't going to make any profit on it," they got within $500 of my offer.

Deal.

I, of course, felt bad that due to helping me with the price, they wouldn't be able to afford steak for dinner in Neverland that night.

Then paperwork.

My salesman said the money guy would get involved, and they'd have to check this and that. I was asked for my permission to do that.

Then the conversation got interesting.

I told him, "Just so you know, I changed my name a couple of months ago. I believe everything has been updated, but if you see a name that doesn't match, that's the reason."

He sounded a little skeptical and said, "Oh, okay," picking up a pen to write. "Do you mind telling me your former name?"

"Stephen."

He didn't look up and said, "Excuse me?"

"My former name was Stephen."

He looked up at me with wide eyes and said in a surprised tone, "Really?"

"Yes. I am one of 'those,'" I said with a smile.

"O...kay." I wasn't sure where this was headed until he finally said, "Please know I'm a supporter."

"I appreciate that. I assumed you knew."

"Why would you think I knew?" he said with genuine curiosity.

"The look you gave me when I turned around out there on the lot."

He lowered his head and said, "I am so sorry that's what you thought. I know I did give you an odd look, but that wasn't the reason. The truth is that when you turned around, I had to look up. I was thinking, why does she get to be so tall? Life is so unfair; I wish I were tall."

We both laughed and chatted a bit about height. He shared that he was 5'7", while I am 6'0". It was a fun conversation.

Eventually, he said, "Do you mind if I ask how long ago...?"

Not letting him finish, I said, "I started HRT a little over a year ago."

"Wow. Do you mind another question?"

"Not at all."

He seemed to be very concerned. "Does it hurt? I always wondered if it hurt."

Making him work a little for it, I asked, "Does what hurt?"

"The changes the hormones put you through," he wasn't sure he should be asking this.

"You do go through a second puberty, so the physical changes that come with that are felt, but I wouldn't describe it as painful. The real pain is in my past."

He smiled and said, "That makes sense. Good for you! I'm very happy for you."

Finally, he went to give paperwork to the money guy. He quickly returned and asked if he could tell the money guy my former name. I told him it didn't bother me at all.

I then moved to the money guy's office, knowing that he knew about me.

Money guy was very nice—nothing exciting, just paperwork and a few questions.

I was sitting across from money guy holding a pen when he slid some paperwork to me and said, "This is a statement that the car we're buying from you was only used for standard transportation; it just means you didn't take the vehicle out drag racing or anything."

I slammed my pen onto his desk and, using my most righteous indignation voice, said, "Just what do you mean by that remark!?"

He seemed a bit unsure and confused, saying, "Oh no, it's just a statement that the car was just used as transportation, and I was joking that you never took it out drag... I'm so sorry..."

I started laughing.

He looked confused and said, "You're laughing; thank goodness you're laughing. I am very sorry. You weren't offended?"

"It's fine. I was just kidding you."

We both laughed.

I love these moments.

beauty parlour . . .

May 12, 2024

It probably comes as no surprise that I love having my "hair done." There were so many years that I fought against my hair—buzzcuts and head shaves were regular occurrences.

My stylist is amazing, her salon is such a welcoming, affirming space.

On my last visit, as she was working her magic, she said, "You are so lucky to have such long eyelashes. It is SO unfair."

Without missing a beat, I said, with all seriousness, "Look, you were born with a vagina, so I think you should be okay with me getting the eyelashes."

She laughed out loud. "Okay, you're right . . . I hope you use that line as much as possible with your cis girlfriends."

I do.

locker room . . .

May 16, 2024

There is a quote from Dustin Hoffman's character in *Tootsie* that I think about often. Michael Dorsey says, ". . . I was a better man with you, as a woman . . . than I ever was with a woman, as a man." The quote doesn't exactly fit with my specific circumstance, but I do believe I am a better person as my true self than I ever was pretending to be something I'm not.

I have had an amazing semester.

I have experienced first-hand so much kindness and grace. Of course, there are occasional bumps in the road here and there, but I am ecstatic that I have so many positive moments that I can share.

Please humor me while I share one more saccharine sweet story from this past semester.

I mentioned in a previous entry that I had one class that was composed primarily of male athletes. As I said, entering the classroom very much felt like I was "walking into a locker room." All the students in the class were respectful, and they were a very fun group from the start.

There was an exception.

One young man in the class made it obvious from day one that he had no interest in a public speaking course (I know, who does?).

He also demonstrated he wasn't particularly thrilled with having me as his professor.

He was never disrespectful, but he wouldn't participate in class discussions, never reacted or played along with my dad humor (I may be trans, but I love a dad joke), etc. You could assume this student was just shy, but I noticed he was always engaged with his teammates, talking and joking around.

He did not like me.

Around the third or fourth week of the semester, I noticed the ice started to crack. He became a little more talkative in class and allowed himself to grin or roll his eyes at my humor.

His first speech was a fairly good performance.

One day in class, I was talking to each student individually about potential topics for their next presentation.

This student had used his sport as the topic of his first speech. He told me it was the only topic he felt comfortable talking about.

I noticed he was wearing a classic "Nirvana" t-shirt and asked him about it. He shared that he loved '80s music. He appeared happy that I was able to discuss this topic with him. He then told me that he got the love of this music from his "very" conservative dad. Dad and son collect '80s vinyl together. (I love this!) I encouraged him to use his love of this music, his favorite band, and/or sharing a cool hobby with his dad as the topic of his next presentation.

From that point on, the ice really started to melt. By midterm, he was participating fully in discussions and offering comments on my amazing jokes.

After midterms, a great moment happened.

He came into my class late; he had run to get there. Because of his running, he had some red spots on his face.

His buddies gave him a hard time about it, with me finally saying, "You know they sell concealer."

In all seriousness, using a "teaching moment" voice, he slowly and methodically responded: "I . . . do . . . *not* . . . wear . . . make-up." It was hilarious—a true performance.

My lame response was, "Well, obviously."

I didn't get the laugh he did.

From that moment forward, he was uninhibited. He reveled in attempts to play-fully jab me whenever the opportunity presented itself.

Two weeks before the end of the semester, he fired his most aggressive shot.

We were working on the "Group Project." Shockingly, students do not generally like this project. During class, a student asked me, "Why do you make us do group work?"

My response was going to be, "I really love that it makes a group of young people that don't always agree have to work together and compromise in order to achieve a goal."

While attempting to deliver that response, I only got out the first three words: "I really love . . ."

A booming voice that was not my own said, "GUYS!"

Laughter and funny shocked "oooohs" from the other students.

I turned to the young man who, only thirteen weeks earlier, had refused to crack a smile at my hilarious jokes, to see him looking out the window, trying desperately to hide his laughing grin.

Using my harshest teacher voice, "Excuse me?"

"What?" he said, reminding me of "Vinnie Barbarino."

"You just said, 'Guys!'"

He broke and started laughing. "I'm sorry; I'm sorry."

I continued, "We wouldn't have a problem if you had said, 'MEN!'"

Trying to be sincere, "Sorry."

Laughter. I wasn't done.

"By the way, have you told your dad about me?"

"Uh, no, I have not," he said sternly.

I took a seat on the desk in front of the classroom, crossed my legs, and using a finger, I started to play with my curls. I then said, with a very coy, sexy voice, "Could you tell your dad about me?"

Brought the house down.

Shaking his head and turning a shade of red, he said, "I give up. I surrender. You win."

When we had our final exam, he asked if he could speak to me after class. I said yes.

After the exam, he asked if I would reconsider giving him partial credit for a late assignment he turned in because he really needed to get a "B" in the course. I told him that I couldn't change that grade, and he wouldn't be getting a "B" in the course.

"I understand," he said. "I want you to know this really became my favorite class this semester." He turned to leave.

The truth is this student had a "B+" average for the course.

Grading a speech presentation is, in so many ways, subjective. I almost always spot a few points on final grades, particularly if the student has put forth genuine effort and shown improvement over the semester.

"I think you've earned an 'A' in the course."

He turned back to me. "Really?" With a huge smile on his face, he continued, "I have learned a lot."

I smiled back at him. "I think you learned a little more than you bargained for."

"What do you mean?"

"I mean the first day I walked into this class, you had made up your mind that you weren't going to like the subject or your professor. But you gave both a chance, and you found that both could be okay."

"You're not wrong." He looked down. "I'm sorry about that."

"Don't be sorry. Just don't forget what you learned."

He looked up and smiled. "I won't."

I love these students.

Representation is important.

progesterone . . .

May 18, 2024

I had to stop by the pharmacy today to pick up a refill for progesterone.

Progesterone aids in trans-feminine patients' breast-shape development.

The pharmacist who has filled all my HRT prescriptions waited on me.

When he returned with my order, I was a little taken aback that he was obviously staring at my chest.

Pointing and waving his finger at my cleavage, he said, "I really like that."

As I was deciding to respond with either, "I beg your pardon" or "Thanks, honey," I glanced down.

I had forgotten that I was wearing my cool retro "Mickey Mouse Club" t-shirt.

Yep... pharmacist guy is a fan... of classic Disney.

THE question . . .

May 22, 2024

In a previous entry I answered some of the questions I've gotten about transition.

I didn't answer THE question.

If you're reading this, you are more than likely not someone who has asked me THE question. I realize that for a lot of people I know I am their first; the first real-life trans person they know. Because of that, I truly appreciate when people ask me questions; how would we ever learn if we didn't ask?

I am always excited to have the opportunity to answer questions. Admittedly, I have been thrown off a couple of times when someone asked THE question.

"Are you going to have **the** surgery?"

"You going to have one of them **sex change** operations?"

"You gonna have **it** done?"

Those are three literal ways I have been asked THE question by people that I would consider casual friends. A very kind and supportive group, but not people I'd say are close friends. I should be happy that for the first time in my life I have so many people interested in what's going on down there.

So, what's the problem?

The best way to address that is to simply ask how you would feel if you were asked about what was going on between your legs in a casual conversation taking place in your office; at a meeting; having lunch; etc.

It wouldn't happen to you, and nor would you ask any cis person those questions.

To put it simply, you shouldn't ask a trans person a personal question that you wouldn't ask anyone else or wouldn't want someone to ask you.

That people can so casually ask a trans woman/trans-feminine person about their genitals is indicative of our patriarchal society. If you haven't noticed, with all the anti-trans legislation/hate being spewed politically, there is half of the trans population that remains virtually invisible: trans men/trans-masculine folks; and yes, they make up half of the trans population.

Why are they ignored?

Because the threat that the cis world feels from the trans community is all about the male member. How could someone born with a penis not want to be a "man"? How could someone born with a phallus reject it — not need or want it? It is simply inconceivable to most cis people; therefore, there is something horribly wrong with trans people.

On the other hand, someone born with a vagina would of course want to be a "man" — who wouldn't? My trans brothers are not seen as any threat to the cis world.

There are a lot of smart people who have written extensively on this topic, and I have grossly oversimplified it here.

I have put some thought into how to best answer THE question when asked by people that shouldn't be asking it.

"I don't know, how about you? Have you had a hysterectomy?"

or

"Of course I am, by the way are you circumcised?"

See what I mean when I say you generally don't ask questions like this casually?

My other thought is to say, "I don't know, but let me tell you what happens during that procedure..."

That doesn't sound so bad, does it?

It seems most people think gender-affirming surgery (GAS) for M-to-F involves some sort of Lorena Bobbitt operation. During the surgery, the penis is not removed; it is cut in half and then... guessing you don't want to hear more... hell, I don't want to hear more

I'm sure you can understand that making the decision to undergo surgery is deeply personal and not something that is taken lightly by any trans person or medical professional in this country. The fantasy that has been sold that children are arbitrarily being given "sex changes" is a horrible lie.

Even as an adult, if I decided to have "bottom" surgery I'd need to be on HRT for at least a year and, at minimum, four medical professionals (my therapist; a psychiatrist; my HRT doctor; and a surgeon) would all have to sign off on it. Nothing about medical transition is easy or taken lightly by anyone.

I guess the point of all this is don't ask THE question of a trans person unless you are very close to them. Understandably, a lot of trans people will be highly offended if you ask — tread at your own risk.

But didn't you say you like getting questions?

I did and, though sometimes surprised by it, I am honestly not personally offended by THE question. I understand and can appreciate the curiosity.

Sooooo... here are some of my answers about surgery/surgeries.

There are a lot of surgical procedures available to trans people. At this point in my transition, I have not had any surgeries, nor do I currently have any planned.

I am lucky that I have never had a visible Adam's apple, so I don't have to worry about the tracheal shave.

There is facial feminization surgery available. Honestly, the only thing I have ever considered is making my giant nose a little smaller. I'm not feeling strongly about acting on it.

I have been very lucky with hormones. Everyone reacts differently to them, and the timeline/results vary significantly between individuals. Doctors will normally require you to wait two years after starting hormones before face or breast surgery can be scheduled so the hormones can work their magic. I have been responding extremely well to estrogen, and my doctor has said that I am "ahead of the game."

Hormones cause fat redistribution that can take years, but I've already gotten fairly good results — face getting rounder; hips and butt filling out — and I am very happy to report that I am not going to want any breast augmentation. In a trans woman's memoir that I read recently, the author stated that her body had reacted quickly to hormones. She was convinced it was because her body wanted/needed the hormones. I like that story, though it is not medically supported.

There is vocal therapy available. I think my voice reveals me more than anything at this point. Sometimes I forget to use my softer voice. I've struggled with it a bit — I can do a nice voice, but I refuse to feel like I'm performing all the time. Hormones can make trans men's voices deeper, but estrogen does nothing for us bass girls. There is vocal cord surgery that limits how low the voice can go — that scares the hell out of me and will not be happening.

I have had multiple laser hair removal treatments — so long, five o'clock shadow!

As far as THE surgery goes, there are different options available. If I were a young person, I am certain I'd want the whole enchilada, but as of now I don't really think that is something that I need or want.

There is a small procedure that I am exploring. Though it is considered bottom surgery, it is not invasive — a simple outpatient thing.

I have made no final decision yet.

If you want the full details, feel free to ask, but I may require you to buy me dinner first.

the stare & the hair . . .

May 25, 2024

I think I've said before that one reason I started writing about my experiences was to share some smiles and hopefully help refute the myth that once a trans person starts presenting authentically, their daily life becomes a hellscape of constant challenges.

I am happy to report that every time I go out shopping or running mundane errands, I end up feeling great joy about myself and the people I encounter.

There are two things that I now expect every time I go out in public. One is a little off-putting, and the other makes my vanity very happy.

This double phenomenon is "the stare and the hair."

the STARE...

It is amazing that this happens so regularly. I have rarely noticed it happening multiple times during a single trip. Sometimes the eyes belong to a man, sometimes a woman. Age, socioeconomic factors, location, etc., seem to offer no clues on these people — it can be anybody.

The stare is exactly what it sounds like. Someone locks their eyes on me, and then they hold the gaze for an uncomfortable amount of time. There is no smile or wink, just eyes worthy of a Keane painting.

I used to assume that this happened because they know I am a trans person, and they must be thinking, "Hey, look at that dude in a dress!" The truth is I have no idea what prompts the stare, and that is what makes it particularly creepy.

I like to think that at this point I am passable enough in the real world that if someone suspects me ("suspects me," how weird), there isn't enough evidence for them to be sure. It feels like a pretty good place to be. Perhaps the starer is someone that just senses "something off" about me, like a trans-seeking empath, or someone like my mother, who would say, "You can't fool me — I've got ESPN!" The look could be an attempt to figure me out.

I have a couple friends that have tried to convince me that it happens because "tall girls get looked at." There is no denying that I am a big girl (in more ways than one!), so it could be the reason for some of the looks I get. Or it could be what I am wearing, my jewelry, my eyes, etc. It doesn't matter; it just feels strange.

The stare is certainly not exclusive to me. I've talked to other trans people who have experienced the same thing. There is certainly a possibility that I've always gotten "the stare" and just notice it more now that I am more aware of the environment and my place in it.

There was a time several weeks ago when I decided to stare back.

I am very nostalgic about grocery stores. I started working in a neighborhood market when I was in the sixth grade and worked there until I completed my associate's degree. I was a twenty-year-old that had worked at the same place for nine years. That job was one of my only connections I had with my dad as a child because he had worked in the "general store" that was across the street from his childhood home when he was growing up.

My father loved a grocery store. It sounds strange to most people, but my dad loved to just walk around a store; he'd just stop at one, not needing anything, and just peruse the aisles. My mother forbade him from going with her to do the actual grocery shopping because he would spend too much time "just lookin'." She also refused to send him to pick up things at the store, as he'd always come home with "somethin' new." I was the only one in my family that didn't mind going with him; of course, I'd usually get a "piece a candy" (candy bar) out of the deal.

I like a grocery store.

I am a creature of habit and always follow the same path when I go grocery shopping. I rarely take a list with me and just follow my same route and pick things up as I see them.

I was shopping one day, picking up what are my essentials. Unlike most people, I start in the dairy section. Shopping at a leisurely pace, enjoying people-watching, and trying not to get crushed by the employees shopping for "pick-up" customers. I was wearing a pair of capri pants, a nice blouse, flats, hair, and basic make-up. Nothing special, but presentable.

I reached in for a half gallon of 2% milk. When I turned back to my cart (also known as a buggy in these parts), a short, unkempt woman was a couple of feet from my cart, staring at me. I smiled.

I moved to the egg section, reached in for a dozen. When I turned back to the cart, she was there again. Staring.

I offered a quick smile and moved on to cheese. I reached in for shredded cheese and turned back, and there she was again. I offered another smile but got nothing in return.

"Okay," I thought, "this is a little creepy and ruining my fun." I decided I would reverse course and continue my shopping on the other side of the store — out of order.

I started making my way to the other side to continue my shopping. Suddenly I stopped in my tracks. Why was I letting this person, who doesn't know me or anything about me, dictate where I was going? How dare I allow her to make me uncomfortable shopping for groceries. No way am I going to give a stranger that power over me. In fact, maybe she should know how it feels.

I turned around and headed back to the dairy aisle.

She was still there. I moved my cart in front of hers as she was looking at something. She took her head out of the cooler, and there I was. Staring. A grin on my lipsticked lips. No doubt a sparkle in my eye. Every time she moved and stopped to look at something, I positioned myself so when she looked up she saw my beautiful eyes.

Success!

She was very uncomfortable. She worked very hard to not look up. If she accidentally caught my eye, she would do a nervous shuffle to get out of my view, looking away as if I wasn't there.

Then it hit me. I felt bad. A childish move on my part. I started thinking, "What if she had some sort of mental challenge that wasn't visible?" Could that be why she stared? Not really my finest hour. Admittedly, though, it felt good that I thought I had taken back a bit of power for a moment.

I headed back to the other side of the store, hoping I hadn't traumatized an already potentially traumatized woman.

and the HAIR...

I have very curly hair.

The other thing that is a regular occurrence when I go out is actually very sweet and kind. It does wonders for my ego. I hope you'll forgive me for discussing it.

Women are very generous in sharing compliments about your outfit, jewelry, perfume, etc. I get those compliments occasionally, but there is one compliment I get on a regular basis — my hair. If you or someone you know has curly hair, I bet they will tell you the same thing. Getting a compliment about my hair can make my day. It can also get a bit awkward when a stranger asks if they can touch it — yes, it happens.

One of the best things about transitioning is I finally get to embrace my hair. That sounds like an odd statement to make, but the truth is curly hair is a lot of work. As a kid, my parents fought my curls. My dad always complained that my hair was always a mess. He would constantly insist that I put some "hair oil" on it to get it to lay flat, and when it didn't, he'd threaten me with a buzzcut. It is very strange that he would not like my hair because he is the source of my curls. Growing up, his nickname was "Curly" because of his wavy hair; his best friend's nickname was "Fuzzy" because he always wore a crewcut; they had another buddy nicknamed "Goat," but trust me, it didn't mean "Greatest of All Time" in those days.

Straight (haired) people don't get curly hair.

It will not be controlled; it seriously has a mind of its own. You also need a stylist that knows how to cut it. There are many great stylists who don't know curls. If you're lucky, you will find one that specializes in curls, but you'll pay a hefty price for their services. In the past year, I've paid up because I am done with years of bad haircuts that looked okay the day of but were a complete train wreck every day afterward. When I was a kid, I was always taken to barbers who had the perfect solution: always cut the curl out of it, leaving a misshaped, frizzy mess. Yep. Nevermore. I thoroughly enjoy my hair now.

It's fitting that, with the nightmare that was my hair growing up, it is the source of one of my earliest dysphoric/affirming moments. My grandmother (Granny), who passed when I was in the second grade, would always run her hand through my hair and say, "Your hair is way too pretty to be on a boy."

She would also tell me, "No one will like you if you smell like pee," as an incentive to stop bedwetting.

I'd like to think she'd be proud on both counts now.

While shopping a few weeks ago, I had a hair encounter:

It was beautiful. Lightweight cotton; off-white with large gold polka dots; straight hem across the front well above the knee but below the knee on the sides and back, full with lots of fabric to play with; mid-length sleeves gathered to create a puffy look; made and styled in India; available in my size; and very affordably priced...

But the voice in my head wasn't having it:

Don't you think it's way too young?

The style is unusual; won't it draw unnecessary attention?

Do I really need it? I mean, will I have an occasion to wear it?

I owned nothing like it.

The debate going on in my head was suddenly interrupted by a booming southern woman's voice — a sweet voice that had obviously been altered by years of cigarette smoking.

She was at least my age, if not older, and had obviously lived more than I have. She was shorter than I, but a little heavier. She wore large-frame glasses that made it look like a giant butterfly had landed on her face. Her hair was going gray, straight, with a clip holding it up in the back. I'm never sure if someone is speaking to me in these situations, but she was close enough to me that I had no doubt I was being addressed.

"Honey, you have picked up that dress four times! G'on and get it for goodness' sake."

I was too embarrassed that she was right about my picking it up four times to think about why she'd been watching me.

I smiled at her and said, "I just can't make up my mind." I put the dress back on the rack for the fourth time.

She did that smoker's thing of starting to laugh, but it quickly evolves into a cough.

While fighting the hacking, she managed to get out, "I know whatcha mean, girl; I've picked it up twice myself, but it'll look much cuter on you than on me."

"I don't know about that," I said as she got her hacking under control.

She bellowed, "I do! If I had that hair, I'd sure as heck buy it. It'll look good with your hair."

Feeling modest, I responded, "Well, thank you. You are very kind."

"Honey, I just wish I had your hair," she said as the word hair devolved into another smoker's hack.

The off-white, gold polka-dot dress from India currently resides in my closet.

dysphoria . . .

June 4, 2024

dysphoria – noun – dys·pho·ria – a state of feeling very unhappy, uneasy, or dissatisfied (Merriam-Webster).

Gender dysphoria is the diagnosis that trans people get. It is specifically the issues associated with what your gender is, as opposed to what sex the doctor checked on your birth certificate based on your anatomy when you were born.

A great many trans people develop crippling depression because of dysphoria. I have never felt that I was depressed, either as a child or as an adult. Dysphoria did result in my isolating myself significantly from others.

In childhood, I always felt like an "old soul" that my peers just hadn't caught up to yet. I believed that was the reason I always felt like I didn't fit in with them. The goalpost would always shift as I'd tell myself it'd be different when I got to high school... college... my first adult job... etc.

It's funny looking back on my life that I wasn't a lonely kid, but I was a loner. I often really enjoyed being by myself. I still do. I certainly always had friends and think, for the most part, I was well-liked (yes, very Willy Loman...).

Having no interest in sports, girls, cars, or alcohol, and having a job made it easy to isolate myself in my teenage years. Don't get me wrong — I had people I was "close" to, but that could only go so far before the wall went up.

Gender dysphoria can make an appearance at any time in someone's life. It is thought to be most common when puberty starts changing the body. For me, it started as early as I can remember. Of course, growing up I had no clue what dysphoria was, much less that it was what I was feeling.

There are distinctive moments from my early years that have always stood out to me. They are clear examples of gender dysphoria — moments where I knew I was different, but not necessarily how or why.

I suppose my earliest memory that would indicate dysphoria is one I've already shared: my grandmother telling me my hair was "too pretty to be on a boy." I think most boys in the age group that I was at the time would be horrified to be told anything about them was "too pretty." I loved it. I would just smile and say, "Thank you."

My next clear memory is from kindergarten. Our class got a new playhouse about halfway through the year. It was spectacular; it had two levels. There is absolutely no way it would be permitted in a classroom today, as the second level would correctly be seen as a serious accident waiting to happen.

The first level was a play kitchen — stove, refrigerator, sink, cabinets, kitchen table, and fold-down ironing board. The second level was basically just an open space, about 12' x 12' carpeted area. Only five students were allowed to play in the kitchen at any given time, with only two allowed on the second floor. The boys all wanted on the second level, while all the girls wanted in the kitchen.

I hated the second level.

The only access to it was a straight ladder built into the playhouse, consisting of metal bars that would roll under your feet when you attempted to climb. Once on the upper level, the whole thing shook like crazy. The only thing to do once braving the death ladder was to sit on pillows or just look down on the rest of the classroom. Boring. But there were a million things that needed to be done in the kitchen! I loved playing in the kitchen so much.

One day, while shopping with my mother, she came to find me in the toy section. In those days, it was normal that when you went to a department store with your parent, you'd be dropped off in the toy department. They would retrieve you when they were done shopping. When she found me that day, I begged her to buy me a toy iron. She was a bit surprised by my request. I told her we needed it for our classroom kitchen. Because it was inexpensive, and it was a very rare occurrence that I asked for a new toy, she purchased the tin iron. I spent a lot of time ironing in that kitchen (seriously, I was born to play "Edna" in *Hairspray*). You know you're old when you now see the exact model toy tin iron that you played with as a child for sale in antique stores.

Another kindergarten memory: we had a project in which we had to make a "suit-case" out of construction paper. Basically, just a flat envelope that we decorated like a suitcase. We were told we were going to take a trip; I don't remember the location or if we could pick our own destination. The teacher brought in a pile of magazines and catalogs, and we had to "pack" our suitcases for our trip by cutting out what we needed from the pictures in those publications.

The teacher collected our luggage and, like an overzealous airport security agent, rifled through our belongings in front of the whole class. I got laughed at because I was the only student that had "packed" underwear. She commended me for remembering to pack essentials but quickly returned them to my luggage when someone pointed out they were "girl" underwear. I don't think I consciously picked out a pair of girl's briefs; I just did.

Another brief encounter I remember happened in the first grade. Classic 1970s school playgrounds included another lawsuit-waiting-to-happen appara-tus known as the "monkey bars." They were a series of steel bars clamped together, allowing kids to climb on them like monkeys. Our playground had an enormous setup that had to be 14' to 16' tall.

There was one girl in my class that was a true tomboy. She always played and roughhoused with the boys. One day her mother sent her to school in a beautiful party dress. I was mesmerized by it. At recess, the boys were playing on the monkey bars; she joined them. I made my way to the monkey bars that day because I wanted to watch the dress. She did not hold back on playing because of her attire.

Soon she had hooked her knees across one of the bars and flipped upside down. When her skirt dropped down, the most amazing thing I'd seen up to that point was revealed — a pair of lavender panties that matched her dress, with row after row of gathered lace.

The boys all laughed and made fun of her.

I did not.

All I could think was, "Why didn't I have amazing underwear like that?"

My friends through elementary school and most of junior high (that's middle school for you young'ins) were girls. So much so that some of my family would kid me about how much of a "ladies' man" I was going to be. Yeah, I know... right?

My most vivid memory of a moment in junior high happened in the locker room after gym class — because of course it did.

There were a couple of boys who were further along in development than most of us: they had hairy underarms. As we were changing, they started harassing their friend, who was still very smooth. They kept laughing and calling him "girl pits." When I heard this, I checked my own underarms — not hairy, but a dusting of fuzz.

That afternoon, when I got off the bus, I went in our house, put my books down, and went straight to the bathroom. Within minutes, I too had "girl pits." I'll never know if my dad noticed any fuzz stuck in his razor the next time he shaved.

The thing that always strikes me about this and other situations is that I never really thought about it. I didn't tell myself that when I got home, I was going to do this. I just did it.

All through my childhood, I was a true connoisseur of television. I loved watching it, reading about it, and talking about it.

Everyone always thought I had a huge crush on "Samantha Stephens" from *Bewitched* and that I always wanted to be "Gopher" from *The Love Boat.* The truth was I wanted to be "Samantha Stephens" — I can still do the nose twitch — and I had a huge crush on "Gopher" — I know some of you will laugh at that, but he was so cute.

"Corporal Klinger" on *M*A*S*H* held my interest for his brave fashion choices and the relative acceptance of his chosen look.

Television in the '70s and early '80s was really my only source of information for "alternative lifestyles." Luckily, my parents never censored what I watched.

I was a loyal fan of the Norman Lear comedies *All in the Family, Maude, The Jeffersons, Good Times,* and *One Day at a Time.* Those shows at one point all featured stories about gay people or people that had "sex changes" (a common term in those days). If you've never seen the "Beverly LaSalle" episodes of *All in the Family*, I highly recommend watching them. Particularly moving is the two-part episode "Edith's Crisis of Faith."

I'm very grateful I had those representations to watch in those days.

My high school years were my sexual awakening. I started to accept that I was "gay." I certainly didn't "come out" in any way back then. The conservative backlash against the '70s and the AIDS epidemic raging made it even more difficult.

In high school, if I went to a movie with male friends, we couldn't sit beside each other. We had to be separated by an empty seat or else we'd be "gay." You could have a single earring, but if it was in the wrong ear, you were "gay."

That kind of highly intelligent thinking was rampant.

Since I had primarily been close to girls, I lost most of my friends. They, like me, became very interested in boys, and they, unlike me, could act on their interest. I became a third wheel — always a difficult position, but particularly unpleasant as a teenager.

There were a couple of effeminate boys in school, but I never felt particularly connected to them. I don't believe I presented particularly feminine growing up. That is not unusual for a trans person, as the idea of presenting as expected is ingrained in us.

I had crushes on some of my classmates but always kept it under wraps.

There was one peer that I was crazy about. Dark hair, brooding artist type. A "bad boy" that was always quiet. He always went out of his way to be nice to me (swoon). Parachute pants were a thing back then. One day he came to school wearing a pair of white parachute pants — white parachute pants with black briefs underneath. I thought I was going to pass out before he got sent home.

I was always enthralled (jealous) when the cheerleaders got to wear their uniforms to school. The boys would act so goofy (cute) trying to glimpse the dance panties underneath.

Perhaps they were like me in elementary school, wondering why their own underwear wasn't as interesting.

honey . . .

June 9, 2024

I made it back from a trip to Florida—a rather lengthy jaunt that clocks in at around twelve hours one way. I enjoy driving. My preference is to travel at night; hitting Atlanta is so much nicer in the middle of the night as opposed to the middle of the day.

Traveling alone is fun and therapeutic for me, though there is another layer of risk added, which I am more keenly aware of now.

I am happy to report I faced no issues to be concerned about on my trip. I peed like a queen at every stop. In all the restrooms I visited, no one, to my knowledge, was harassed, intimidated, molested, indoctrinated, or groomed because of my presence. I managed to go in, do my business, wash my hands, and leave without incident.

I did break the law in Florida: I used the ladies' room in a state-owned rest stop. I've waited so many years to be a "bad girl."

On the way home last night, I stopped at a Travel Truck Stop in the middle of nowhere, Georgia. No bathroom issues at all—again, peed like a queen (yeah, I might have to use that phrase a lot now).

After I finished not bothering anyone in the restroom, I was waiting in line to pay for a cup of coffee and a bottle of water. There were several customers and just one cashier.

A man in his forties with a backwoods Georgia sort of vibe came up to open the other register. He looked at me and said, "Come over here, honey; I'll take care of you."

I moved to his register.

During the transaction, he called me "honey" or "hon" four additional times.

He scanned my items and said, "That all you need, hon?"

While paying, I was using the "tap" feature on my card. I inadvertently pulled the card away too soon, so the machine didn't read it.

Before I realized what had happened, he reached out and took my card out of my hand. "Let me do it for ya, hon." He held the card over the machine and announced, "There ya go," as he handed my card back.

"You need a bag, hon?"

As I picked up my items and headed out, he said, "You come back to see me, honey."

Not once in all my years presenting as male did I ever call a woman "honey" or "hon."

It is sexist and misogynistic.

My first thought was that I should say something to him.

I didn't.

The truth is, the relatively newly released girly girl in me loved it. It is such a powerful and amazing feeling to have your identity affirmed. Even if it is in a sexist way, it was still recognition of my femininity.

Can I have it both ways? That question seems to be a bit of a recurring theme...

passing mister . . . uh muster . . .

June 14, 2024

I have shared before that one of the reasons I waited so long to begin transitioning was my concern about passing. If I couldn't pass, then my life would surely be a living hell.

I was certain I'd be ridiculed daily and cast out of all social situations.

This is certainly not an unusual concern for trans people. Some worry every time they go out that they'll be "clocked"—called out as our supposed "biological" sex by someone in public. For many, this can ruin their day or be absolutely devastating.

During the pandemic, when I was considering my options about living authentically, one thing I needed to answer was if I could handle not being able to pass. Could I survive being "clocked" daily?

I made the decision to go out one day dressed as my feminine self.

I knew I was not passable. Oh, I had a nice dress, accessories, shoes, but I also still had male eyewear, visible beard stubble, and though my hair was growing out nicely, it really wasn't a feminine style.

I went to Walmart in a neighboring town. Though only about twenty miles away, it is in another state. Of course, I was nervous but persevered. I was met with lots of stares and smiles.

I was very nervous, but it was incredibly liberating. It felt amazing being dressed, my head held high, not giving a damn what anybody else thought about me.

As I shopped that day, there were two incidents that truly tested me.

At one point, I passed an aisle and looked down it to see a man who looked up at me. I continued but soon realized he had started following me. I cut down an aisle here and there, but he didn't relent. I suddenly felt very nervous.

Then a thought crossed my mind. He appeared to be about six inches or so shorter than I and slighter in build. I remembered what I had learned as a high school teacher: if there is a student fight and the participants are boys, you can break it up rather easily; boys generally do not want to fight because they don't want to risk getting their ass kicked in front of everybody. On the other hand, if it is two girls, then the best option is to get the hell out of the way because they are going for blood.

What was this guy going to do in Walmart?

I led him to an "action alley" in the store, stopped my cart, turned around, and just stared at him. Perhaps this was the genesis of developing a pattern of returning Walmart stares. He stopped, very surprised, and then lowered his head and slinked away. I didn't see him again.

A friend reminded me later that if I transitioned, I would have to get used to things like that because "women deal with this sort of thing all the time."

I am very much aware of the dangers I can face as a trans person and attempt to take precautions. My tactic of basically confronting that guy will often not be the best option. The funny thing is that if Stephen had ever found himself in a similar situation, I don't think he would have reacted in the same manner. It's fitting that

I've discovered that in so many ways, Deanna is much smarter and more confident than Stephen was.

The other encounter that day was when a cis couple raced out of an aisle and almost ran into me.

When I passed in front of them, the woman loudly said to her partner, "You know what THAT is, don't you?"

I turned around and smiled as the man just gave a shrug.

This entire experience left me exhilarated and filled me with a confidence I hadn't felt before. I can't really say that I made the decision to transition that day, but it certainly was influential. I learned the most amazing thing—it just did not matter if I "passed" or not. Talk about an epiphany.

Living authentically was the only thing I needed.

But wait a tick... aren't you doing everything you can to pass? Makeup, hairstylist, hormones, name change, pronouns—aren't you doing that so you'll pass?

No.

Transitioning is and should be a completely selfish act.

It is one hundred percent self-care. The hysteria about trans people spread today in the media is all about "it" being done to someone or that transitioning is about taking something away from another group. I still haven't received my copy of the much-lauded "Trans-agenda" from headquarters. For the person transitioning, it is about one thing: choosing to feel alive as opposed to experiencing life feeling like a member of the walking dead.

Yes, I have my hair and nails done. Yes, I wear makeup. I do these things for the same reason a cis woman does—because she likes it. It makes her feel good, confident... and attractive.

Hormones are amazing.

Yes, there are physical changes that help people like me pass. Those changes are lovely. But the true magic is in the things that only I get to experience. The emotions, the smooth skin, not smelling like a goat, the change in libido, the orgasms (gentlemen, you honestly have NO idea), etc., are the reasons for HRT.

Just feeling happy to be me; to be alive.

My feminine name and pronouns make life easier as they help to put people I interact with more at ease. But the goal is to be seen and respected as the person I am—and nothing else.

It does have to be acknowledged that it is literally a safer world for those trans people who pass.

I feel very fortunate that I don't get "clocked" often in public situations. As I've said before, I feel I am "close enough" that someone may question, but they aren't confident or interested enough to publicly comment on their suspicions. Perhaps people are just being nice... yes, there's my old friend "imposter syndrome"... perhaps I'll discuss him in the future.

If I am "clocked," it is usually by someone addressing me as "sir."

I don't let this bother me for several reasons. It seems mostly to be associated with when they are focused on my voice—on the phone or in a speaker situation. Voice is one of the most crucial characteristics we use subconsciously to identify sex in social situations. When addressed as "sir," I have yet to feel it was someone trying to be disrespectful. It is a normal thing for someone to misuse "sir;" we all make mistakes.

The reality is that many cis people have dealt with being accidentally misgendered like this their entire lives. If the worst thing that happens to me on any given day is I get called "sir," then that day goes in the win column.

I have also been a big fan of the STAR TREK approach—where all people are addressed as "sir" when showing respect.

I have honestly only corrected one person (so far) for using a "wrong" gender address. I was on the phone with a company and was asked my name (Deanna) and then to spell it (D-E-A-N-N-A).

After providing my name and spelling it, the rep said, "Thank you, sir."

Really?

I asked the representative to repeat my name and then requested I not be called "sir."

They apologized and called me "ma'am" for the rest of the call.

Please always remember that my story is mine; everyone's journey is different.

fired . . .

June 26, 2024

A couple of firsts to report for Deanna.

The first "first" to report is something Stephen never managed to accomplish.

I was fired today.

PRU (Poorly Run University) nevermore . . .

PRU HR prefers to say I was "permanently laid off."

I will not spend a lot of time bellyaching about this development, as I've suspected my demise was imminent for some time. There were twelve professors given our walking papers today. I suspect more will be on the way.

The biggest difference between working in a public university versus a private one is that a private university can go bankrupt—particularly when under the guidance of inept administrators.

If you want to hear the dirty details, I'll be happy to rant and rave a bit for you privately, but honestly, I'm fine.

I will sincerely say I will miss the PRU students. I will always consider it such an honor to work with young people.

So, what's next, hot shot?

I don't have all the answers, but I do already have a new job!

The first time I've been hired as Deanna!

I will be working at BTMC (Big Time Medical Center) as an SP (standardized patient.) Medical students are put through simulations with "real" (standardized) patients. The job is part-time.

Acting, communication, serving students, etc.—all are involved.

As some of my trans brothers and sisters know, many medical professionals have no idea how to deal with a trans person, most often because they have never had the opportunity. They seem excited about having me, and I feel that I'll be doing something important.

During the application process, I've felt so excited and energized being in this new environment.

It's nice to feel appreciated.

So: fired . . . hired . . . I am very lucky.

got to be a mom . . .

June 28, 2024

Today I had to finish up some business with my parents' estate. The man assisting me was very nice and helpful.

It feels a bit weird in situations like this because I never know if someone knows I am a trans person or not. Don't get me wrong—it doesn't matter, and I truly don't care.

I did know that today's business was going to include paperwork identifying me as "Stephen." I knew I was going to have to "out" myself to someone at some point in the process.

"Hi, I'm Deanna; trans person; formerly Stephen; nice to meet you," isn't something I ever feel I should lead with.

I wasn't even sure this guy was the one I'd need to explain my situation to ultimately.

While waiting on someone to bring some forms to him, we chatted a bit.

There were pictures on his desk of his family, which I commented on: "Beautiful family . . ."

He then started talking about his kids, as any proud dad would.

Finally, he said, "So how about you—how many do you have? You've got to be a mom."

OMG!

I was in a combined state of shock and bliss. What a huge compliment.

Later I thought about how much I loved his comment, but also how can this man have no clue what a dangerous thing that could be to ask someone. What if I'd been someone who wanted children and couldn't have them—or worse, had lost a child? Triggers can be so powerful.

I guess I was triggered in a good way, because his comment reminded me of something one of my athletes said this past semester: "You smell like my mom."

Perhaps I'm more matronly than I've realized.

"So how about you—how many do you have? You've got to be a mom."

I answered, "No, I don't have any."

He quickly—and wisely—moved on to another subject.

He had no idea I am a trans person.

We finally got to the necessary paperwork. He was looking over some of the details when he suddenly stopped. He shuffled through a couple of pages like he was looking for something, then stopped and looked up.

"So Deanna, Stephen is your husband?"

I almost laughed out loud—but didn't.

Without skipping a beat, I said, "No, I used to be Stephen."

I pulled out the paperwork documenting my change.

He looked stunned. He just stared at me.

"Here is the paperwork that proves who I am. If you still want to do business."

He broke his stare and said, "Oh my god, I am so sorry. I didn't mean to be rude. I was . . . I was just a little surprised. I had NO idea."

"That's fine. It's not a problem."

"Again, I am sorry, but WOW."

"It's really okay."

We finished our business without any further triggers or shocks.

compliment . . .

July 3, 2024

I've said it before, but I am always surprised at how nice and free women are with compliments.

I'm often unsure of my looks—my hair and my outfits.

Is it too young for me?

Is it too tight?

Is this lip stick too much?

I was feeling a little overwhelmed today but had my day made by four people commenting on the blouse I was wearing.

The lady behind the counter at the pharmacy even said, "You always wear the cutest tops!"

I also got two compliments on my hair.

Never underestimate the power of being kind to someone . . . or maybe I'm just easy . . .

questions pt.2 . . .

July 7, 2024

Sharing a few more answers to questions I've gotten.

As always, please know these are my personal feelings and observations.

Everyone's journey is different, and I make no judgment on those that may feel differently about some of these things.

"You're on hormones so you'll never have to deal with menopause?"

Maybe.

The first several years on hormones the idea is to get the numbers high so that the physical and emotional changes get going full force. It is basically going through a second puberty. Once I have been at the higher level for a period of time, the doctor will start to back the hormones down, so my levels are "comparable to a woman my age." When that happens, it is possible that I'll experience some menopausal symptoms.

My cis friend who has been dealing with menopause said to me, "enough with this youth shit, it's time for you to have hot flashes!"

"What was the biggest surprise you got since starting on estrogen?"

I read all about the things to expect when starting, so I guess there wasn't a true surprise.

The surprise is more in the experience and/or degree of the change.

I think for me the one that continually amazes me is the change in skin. "Skin will get softer" is on the list of effects of estrogen. My skin was one of the earliest changes I noticed as it did get softer. It seems to continuously get softer and softer.

With that softening, it has gotten more sensitive too. As a male I rarely got cold, but now I get the chills regularly.

There is another amazing surprise that answers another sometimes awkward question . . .

"Are orgasms really that different?"

YES. . . YES . . . OH GOD . . . OH GOD, YES . . . ETC. ETC. . . .

I was certainly skeptical when I read "will experience orgasms differently." It truly is amazing what hormones do in our bodies.

Without getting too graphic . . .

As a male I experienced it as an amazing moment centered in one area of the body. On hormones, the experience is much more spread out—both longer and location. Pleasure in multiple areas of the body is set off.

Yeah . . . it's VERY nice.

"I've heard some right-wing nut jobs say that trans women are just acting out some sexual fantasy. Is that true?"

There is no doubt fetish associated with cross-dressing, but just like drag, being trans and/or nonbinary is a VERY different thing.

No one is going to put themselves through transition "just for fun."

Also, I doubt it will come as a surprise to anyone that being on estrogen significantly reduces the sex drive.

"What was it like telling your friends?"

I never really worried that I'd lose any of my friends because I am trans, but I was a little nervous when sharing the news.

I was more surprised that they were surprised. I had assumed their reaction would be, "well duh, that tracks."

For the most part the reaction was "okay." Some discussed concerns for safety and livelihood.

I was taken aback at how little most knew in general about trans people. My closest friends are like-minded liberals, but multiple people reacted with, "So, you're a drag queen?"

Uh, no.

One friend said she fully supported me but didn't understand a thing about it. She asked what the simplest way would be that I could explain it. She was the one that asked if I were a drag queen, so I told her that for me being trans is the opposite of that. I told her that basically I had spent most of my life feeling as if I were forced to do male drag every day.

She liked that explanation.

I told most of my closest friends right before I started HRT.

One friend I didn't get a chance to tell until six weeks into it.

When I saw her, she asked, "What are you doing different? Your skin looks great; you're almost glowing."

I said, "I have something I want to tell you."

She said, "You're transitioning!"

That was nice.

One of the biggest surprises I got early on was when a stranger I hadn't told, told me.

I had been on hormones for a couple of months and was still very much in what I considered my androgynous phase. My parents were both in the long-term care facility then, and I was having to deal with a lot of their business. I had gone to the bank to do some things.

Sitting across from the banker, we finished our business, and she said, "I hope you don't mind my saying this, but I want you to know I am so proud of you."

"Um . . . thanks, but what are you talking about?"

She looked me straight in the eye and said, "You're transitioning, and that's amazing."

I almost fell out of my chair. "How did you . . . "

"I can see it. My wife used to be my husband."

She went on to share a bit about her situation. Her best line was, "I never knew I was a lesbian, but damn I'm a great big one!" She has continued helping me out many times with banking issues, and I now consider her a good friend.

"Would a man ever be interested in dating a trans woman/feminine person?"

The answer is you'd probably be surprised.

I honestly have had more dating opportunities as a trans person than I ever had as a "gay male."

It certainly comes with added challenges.

Believe it or not, I get regular proposals from people in some trans chat rooms.

I've had multiple offers of free trips to NYC and London to spend a weekend with someone.

"No way, you're kidding!"

I'm not.

The reality is these offers are from people who don't know me—only that I am trans. These folks are known as chasers, and they are an extremely dangerous breed.

Chasers are not limited to just men.

Chasers are only interested in someone because they are trans. The attraction/obsession is just wanting to be with someone who is trans. They have zero interest in the person you are. They are usually masters at making you feel like you're something special almost immediately.

Relationships with chasers very quickly enter the abusive realm.

Having dealt with a sociopath several years ago, I am hopefully wise to these shenanigans. I've yet to be tempted to board a plane to meet a stranger.

"Chasers, are they your only option?"

Thankfully no.

Men exist who have no issue seeing me as female.

Pansexuals exist.

There are also a lot of men who have a powerful attraction to femininity. As a trans person, I strive to be very feminine. There are men that appreciate and are drawn to that.

That can get some trans folk into trouble too.

The desire to be as feminine as possible leads some to take the role of a truly submissive person in a relationship. It's easy to see how this can evolve into an abusive situation.

A very common stereotype for trans women/feminine people is that we are totally submissive. This is based on the binary notion that anybody that would willingly give up their "manhood" to be feminine would have to be a weak person. Make that assumption about a trans woman at your own risk.

On that same subject, I have had many kind people tell me how "brave" I am.

I always struggle a bit with that idea. If I am "brave" now, then that would mean I have been a coward most of my life.

I'm not particularly thrilled with that thought.

I do see trans and non-binary people that I think are very brave to embrace their authenticity regardless of the consequences.

I just don't feel that for myself.

I think I feel that way because being Deanna is just so natural and easy for me. It doesn't feel like an act of defiance or something that is brave—just being me.

"Would you ever date someone without telling them?"

No, I would not.

I honestly don't hide who/what I am—"Stephen" is still on my Facebook account. I usually work under the assumption that people know or at least suspect.

I would not be at all comfortable or think someone would appreciate my trying to keep that a secret. I just wouldn't feel right not sharing that with a potential partner.

There is also a safety concern in not revealing yourself to a potential romantic interest. Safety must be a constant consideration for any trans person.

"Anything you miss about being a dude?"

No.

I am at a point in transition that when I see or interact with men, I find it hard to believe I ever tried to be "that" or even that anyone ever thought I was "that."

There is a disconnect with the male world now.

More specifically, there is a real disconnect between Stephen and Deanna.

Nothing I miss, though I will readily admit that standing to pee is decidedly more efficient.

forever stephen . . .

July 12, 2024

I have repeatedly stated that passing was not the goal of my transition, and that having the realization that it ultimately didn't matter was the key to my finding joy.

I will readily and freely admit that it feels amazing when I do pass.

There is a rush of validation and euphoria that fills me when someone just accepts me.

There is a group of people in my life who will likely never see the real me. To them, regardless of any changes, I will be "forever Stephen."

I think that these folks have just known me for too long as that "guy," and now my interactions with them as Deanna are very limited. It would be difficult for them to change.

Ultimately, it falls on me to choose to tell them who I am and how I want to be addressed, but honestly, I have no desire to explain myself to them. I've wondered if maybe on some level I just want to keep that connection to the past.

My parents' house is in a neighborhood that was built in the 1950s. It is a small house in the center lot on our street. Over the years, many families have moved in and out of the neighborhood, but oddly both my current neighbors are people I have known my entire life. The parents have all passed, but all three houses are still owned/occupied by their children.

I was the baby out of all three houses, with my neighbors' kids being a little older than my oldest brother. They were always part of my life, but I was just an annoying "kid" to them while they were friends to my older siblings.

On one side, there were two kids.

The youngest, a daughter, currently lives there. As children, she was very close to my oldest brother.

She has an older brother who was eight or nine years older than me. He was the cool bad boy of the neighborhood. He rode a motorbike, had long hair, whiskers, and always seemed to have car grease on his hands, arms, face, and shirt that he'd ripped the sleeves off. I was always a little scared of him, but honestly, if I'd been older, I'd probably have had a major crush on him. When he moved out after high school, he didn't come around much.

The most vivid memory I have of their house is when his sister, who was six years older than me and always reminded me of "Jan Brady," once asked me over to play with her Easy-Bake Oven. I don't remember how old I was, just that I was in heaven. A "girl" toy that, by way of a light bulb, allowed you to eat baked goods—what's not to love?

She only asked me the one time, though I hinted about it many times afterward.

She was a bit "wild" in her teenage years. She and my oldest brother were known to experiment with cigarettes, alcohol, etc.

After she graduated high school, she just stayed at home. She has never had a regular job. Her mother did alterations for a men's store, and for a while she'd go to work with her as her assistant. That didn't last very long.

For decades, she was rarely seen outside. If she was out and one of my family came out, she would literally run in her house. There, of course, were rumors about what had caused the change. I won't repeat any of them, but you may safely assume they'd make for a good Tennessee Williams play.

Several years ago, she called my mom and was upset and frantic. She had been listening to the radio and heard a song that she swore she had "written." Someone had stolen her song! It's worth noting that she had never been musical or demonstrated any musical talent.

When my mom shared the story with me, I told her she must have been watching Nick-at-Nite.

"WHAT?!?!?"

I shared that the story was a plot on an episode of *The Dick Van Dyke Show* ("Bupkis" Season 4; Episode 24 . . . yeah, I'm that nerd.)

After her father passed, she seemed to be free of some of her demons and has improved a bit.

She now has the vibe of a classic "crazy cat lady."

She was very kind when my parents passed and will speak to me when I see her now. She will occasionally venture into my parent's yard, and it's not uncommon for me to find her crouched down beside my car looking for one of her cats. Yes, it scares the hell out of me.

She has had zero reaction to my being Deanna.

There have been a couple of times that I don't think she realized it was me. When we speak, she always gives me the same odd look that has been the norm for years now.

On the other side is a woman and her husband. The woman is the third out of four kids from that house. She is about twelve years older than me, so to me she has always been an adult. She had two older sisters that I barely remember ever living in the house. She also had a younger brother who is seven years older than me, so he was closer to my older siblings.

The woman and her husband are good neighbors. They have been kind to me. They happily keep an eye on the house between my visits, take care of collecting the mail, and put the trash out on pick-up day if I'm not around.

As mom began losing herself in her last few months, she would get angry at them for silly and paranoid reasons.

An example is the recent *Elvis* movie.

When the movie was released, I wanted to take mom to see it, but she wouldn't go. She talked about it all the time and would ask me when I visited or called, "was it any good?" repeatedly. When the DVD came out, I bought her a copy, and she watched it on a loop.

She knew the neighbor liked Elvis and loaned it to her to watch.

Several days later, mom asked her what she thought.

According to mom, the neighbor said, "It was okay, but I didn't like that they had Elvis cursing. Elvis was Christian, and I just don't believe he'd ever curse."

Mom took this as a personal attack, said something rude, and stormed out.

She never spoke to them again.

Now, that sort of thing would be a normal day for me with mom, but she would never have done that to anybody else if she hadn't been sick.

After she went into the hospital, I talked to them about it, and they understood that it was her sickness.

In my interactions with them, they have obviously noticed my changes.

Often, they'll focus on my shoes or my top but mostly will stay focused on my face, trying not to look anywhere else.

I'm sure they have noticed that most of the mail that comes to my parent's house is addressed to Deanna Haynes.

I'm guessing they won't ever say anything to me about it. I think we are content with a "don't ask; don't tell" policy.

I have wondered if that might change, considering a recent development.

I had been at my parents' house for a few days, and one afternoon I returned from a trip to the store. As I drove past their house, I noticed an old man sitting on the porch.

I waved but then realized I wasn't exactly sure who it was I had waved at.

When I parked my car and came around to the front of the house, the old man was standing in my front yard. It was the younger brother. I hadn't seen him since my brother's funeral over ten years ago.

When he looked at me, his eyes got huge, and he said, "Uh . . . uh . . . Stephen?"

Maybe I should have said, "No, it's Deanna!"

I didn't.

I honestly just didn't feel the need to go into it—plus I had my hands full of grocery bags.

I just said, "Hey, it's good to see you . . . how've you been . . . good to see you . . . etc. . . . ."

He started backing up while we talked and seemed eager to retreat quickly.

I wondered if he might say something to his sister about me and she might be inspired to ask me something.

That was a couple of weeks ago, and we seem to be maintaining our normal "don't ask; don't tell" mode.

I think I can live with it.

Growing up, I think that most everyone thought of me as the "weird one." I was so unlike my siblings and the other kids in the neighborhood.

It wasn't that I was necessarily effeminate, but I think it was obvious to all that I was always following a different beat.

When my neighbors call me "Stephen," it doesn't offend me in any way, but it does feel like they aren't really talking to me.

Weird, right?

I mentioned previously that I was at a point where I was feeling a real disconnect between Stephen and Deanna.

People told me, and I had read, that it would happen, but I wasn't sure at that time what it meant. It is hard to explain, but it's basically that now that Deanna is out and about, Stephen doesn't have to exist anymore.

I don't have to pretend that I am someone I am not or ever was.

the name game . . .

July 19, 2024

My name was legally changed on March 6th. I've covered how smoothly that day went in court, the Social Security office, and the DMV.

I'll now share how it has been dealing with getting everything else in my life changed to Deanna.

I think what has surprised me most about the process is how every organization asks for something different.

When you contact a bank, credit card company, utility, etc., and tell them you need to change your name on your account, they all automatically assume you've gotten married.

They all ask, "What's your new last name?"

Apparently, changing your last name due to marriage is easy and doesn't require the paperwork that someone like me with a name change is required to provide.

I will share a few specific experiences in the name game with companies that I will categorize as THE GOOD, THE BAD, and THE INFURIATING.

Dealing with these companies is certainly not the worst problem to have in the world. I really think it comes down to, "Shouldn't this be easier?"

Why is it more time-consuming to get my name changed on a charge account than it was to literally legally change my name?

In an effort to end on a positive note, I'll cover the worst to the best.

THE INFURIATING

These were no surprise at all in their shabby approach to dealing with a trans name change.

BIG SOUTHERN BANK MORTGAGE

My name was legally changed on March 6th.

On MARCH 8th, I went to a local BSB branch to change the name on the various accounts I hold there. That day they were all changed except the mortgage account, which would have to be done by the mortgage office in Mississippi. All the necessary paperwork was sent to them that day.

I will spare you the number of times I heard the word "inadvertently" from these people.

"We inadvertently forgot . . ."

"We inadvertently neglected to request . . ."

My branch manager got involved multiple times trying to make it happen.

I finally wrote what might be the nastiest letter I've ever written to a company, and with the manager's help, I finally got it done . . . this week . . . JULY 12.

Shameful.

STATE OF TENNESSEE – VITAL RECORDS

This one is a real shocker . . . NOT.

The judge will tell you with your name change that you need to immediately deal with Social Security, driver's license, and apply for an updated birth certificate.

SS and DL = easy breezy.

For an updated birth certificate, you must fill out a form, mail documentation and payment.

I did this and received a letter about two weeks later letting me know they had received the necessary documents and that I could expect my corrected birth certificate to arrive in the mail . . . IN NOVEMBER!

Apparently, someone can open and check the documents, send out a letter confirming, but can't go ahead and take care of the birth record.

I'm sure it's not an intentional, "let's be ***holes about this," or anything.

If you don't know, Tennessee does not allow any gender marker changes, and the corrected birth certificate will be a copy of the original with my birth name "X'd" over old typewriter style, with my new name typed above it.

Stay classy, Tennessee!

THE BAD

Most companies probably fall here, but there is one company in this section that surprised, shocked, and disappointed me.

BIG BOX HOME IMPROVEMENT STORE

No real problems with this one; it was just a clunky, outdated process. They had to snail mail a form to me. I had to fill it out and return it with documentation. Again, no challenges other than it took a bit of time.

BIG BOX COOL RETAILER

I was very disappointed with them, though not necessarily surprised, after they removed PRIDE merchandise from stores last year.

Clunky process, much like BIG BOX HOME IMPROVEMENT STORE, but I had to do it twice. After initially acknowledging they had received the documents, they later claimed to have "lost" them. I had to duplicate the process.

They should probably be on the infuriating list, but those winners were even worse.

THE GOOD

I would have never guessed these two companies would win a place on the "good" list. In fact, I dreaded dealing with both as I assumed they would be a nightmare.

BIG ONE CREDIT CARD

The only credit card company that I was able to change my name on my account with one phone call. I had to digitally send a couple of images of documentation, and they were accepted while still on the call.

The representative was incredibly nice and helpful. When I told him what I was calling about, he immediately started addressing me as ma'am and Ms. Haynes.

A quick/pleasant experience.

BIG CABLE/BROADBAND

Yep, I still find it hard to believe that they were amazing.

When I told the rep what I needed, she responded with a solemn, "oh."

I did my lighthearted, "Yep, I'm one of THOSE."

That usually gets the response, "ok, no problem."

But this lady didn't say that; instead, she said, "Well honey, let me tell you something, you are talking to a true ally, and girl, I'm gonna get you fixed up quick! No worries here, honey!"

It was the quickest change and didn't require any additional documentation.

STILL TO COME

I have a couple I have yet to update my name with, but I haven't worked up the courage . . . I'm talking about you, GIANT HORRIBLE CELL PHONE COMPANY.

aunt joan . . .

July 24, 2024

I have been asked several times if my personality has changed much during transition.

I have been thinking about it quite a bit over the past few weeks. I think it's a pretty tough question to answer, as I don't know how much thought any of us really put into our own personalities.

Obviously, I am more feminine, but for me that isn't really a change—just a freedom I now feel.

One close friend said I was "softer." Which could apply to a lot of things!

Most everyone that is close to me has, of course, mentioned how much happier and confident I seem. I certainly feel that, so I guess that would bring on a nice personality change.

When I began my transition, I decided that I was not going to waste one more day waking up in the morning feeling like I couldn't be me. I would wear what I wanted and act like I wanted.

I now greet each day thankful that Deanna is alive and that she will be freaking fabulous that day. That's a really big change from the past.

A big part of my mindset now is shaped by how I interact with people, knowing they may not approve of me.

Stephen's tendency was always a giant "F" you and a willingness to go into "fight" mode. I certainly never consider myself a "Karen," but Stephen was closer to being one than Deanna has ever been.

Deanna is so much better at showing grace.

I make every effort with my daily encounters to enter them not assuming someone is going to be unkind or intentionally rude because I am a trans person. If someone is unkind, short, or rude, I try to keep the thought that how someone is behaving likely has nothing to do with me. Every one of us has bad days, and it influences how we behave.

We never have any idea what someone is dealing with in their own life.

When I encounter someone that appears to be having a bad day, I just think, "Aren't they lucky to be meeting the 'fabulous' Deanna—how could this not brighten their day?"

The most challenging encounters for me have been the occasions where I must out myself—share with a stranger that I used to be Stephen.

I think I've had to do this more often than normal because of dealing with my parents' estate. Since Stephen was the executor and the beneficiary, I've had to reveal/prove who I am/was on many occasions.

Hopefully, at this point, those days are behind me.

The most recent was at a county office where I had to file my parents' Will for the deed. I had to visit and talk to this office multiple times.

When I revealed that I had been Stephen, there seemed to be a palatable tension that suddenly arose between us. I chose to ignore it and continued being kind, grateful, and hilarious to them.

By the time I was done with my business with them, they were amazing to me, and it clearly didn't matter who/what I was.

On my last visit, they even complimented me on my top, and one lady asked where I had gotten it.

So much of the antagonistic energy aimed at any minority is a complete lack of understanding of that group. Most people at this point don't personally know a trans or non-binary person—not one that they are aware of, anyway.

Most people know nothing about the trans community other than the lies told by talking heads trying to gain something from creating a scary enemy.

I honestly try to use the old "kill 'em with kindness" routine.

I am not looking for a confrontation or a negative experience. I honestly try to give people the benefit of the doubt. I think that all groups— all people—sometimes create negative situations out of what they consider a personal slight.

Again, we have no way of knowing why someone behaves the way they do.

I have found this approach to work most of the time for me.

I was so inspired by the women in the film *Hidden Figures* (highly recommend watching) and how they handled the horrible racism and discrimination thrown at them.

Brilliant, classy, got-shit-done women.

It is an amazing story.

I have worried that my approach makes me a sort of trans "Uncle Tom"—though I guess that would make me an "Aunt Joan" (my therapist loved that one).

Without a doubt, there are times when "fight mode" is unavoidable and appropriate. I am certainly more than capable of it.

There are times that I fail at grace, but I am thankful that I am so much better at it now.

I know it sounds corny and naive, but how much better would our world be with a little more grace in it?

being sir'd . . .

August 28, 2024

Two full days.

Twenty-eight (simulated) doctor's appointments.

Fourteen in person.

Fourteen tele-health.

I am loving this job.

I always do my best to get to work early—mainly because of worry about traffic, and it allows me time to review the project I'm working on that day.

There is a café in the courtyard just outside the building I work in, so usually I just get something to drink and find a place to sit and look over my notes before the day starts.

The place is always busy; employees, students, and hospital visitors keep it packed.

This morning there wasn't a line at the counter and only one employee behind it.

She was working on a plethora of pick-up orders and without looking up said, "I'll be right with you Sir."

Very sweetly, I said, "No problem."

She looked up and said, "Ma'am, I am so sorry. I do that all the time."

I smiled and said, "No worries, I've been called a lot worse."

"It's embarrassing how often I do that."

"I don't think you should worry about it."

I ordered my drink, and when I handed her cash for payment she said, "I love that nail color, it's so pretty."

I said, "Well, thank you, it's what all the BOYS are wearing."

She looked up, completely stone-faced, took a beat, and then relaxed and said, "Oh my god, I love you!"

I said, "I love you too."

We both laughed.

Not all "sirs" are bad.

it went smoothly . . .

September 11, 2024

"I hope it goes smoothly . . ."

"HA, I see what you did there Mr. Funny Guy . . . that's kind of the point of doing it."

This is an entry that may fall into the TMI section of my sharing about my transition journey. If you're not interested in hearing about the medical side of things, then please skip this one.

I had shared some time ago that I wasn't sure where I'd end up on any gender affirming surgeries, but I was considering a "minor" procedure.

It obviously is incorrect to refer to any surgery as minor if it involves being put to sleep and cutting on your body. But the procedure I was considering was an "in and out" afternoon affair, though I would be put under, cut on, and the results would be permanent.

I've had the procedure.

I had an orchiectomy (pronounced orkie-ectomy), often just called an orchie.

Being as old as I am, I always think of *Mork & Mindy* and the "orchie" being something from "Mork's" home planet of Ork. "Mork" did arrive on Earth in an egg-shaped spaceship after all. "NaNu NaNu!"

The procedure is more common than most realize, mainly because people aren't comfortable talking about it. It's common not because of gender care but because of testicular cancer.

An orchiectomy is the removal of the testicles.

That's right—now if someone says to me, "grow a pair!"

I get to say, "been there; done that" or I can point to my chest and say, "working on it!"

Please don't let my snark lead you to believe that all this transition business is a lark.

It is not.

It is literally a life/death subject for many of us trans individuals.

"Everyone's journey is different" is almost a cliche now, but it is the absolute truth. Part of my journey, and the joy I find in it, is seeing humor in it.

My happiness in having someone say to me, "I don't get it" or "It's so weird," is based in the notion that I love the honesty and the questions someone might have about it.

You shouldn't "get it," and you're damn right I'm weird—please God, not JD Vance weird*, but my own brand of weird.

(*I have to say that JD's eyeliner game is to die for though!)

As I have mentioned before, contrary to what some expert Presidential candidates believe, having a gender affirming surgery is not an easy process.

If only I could have gone to school one day and come home having the surgery all wrapped up!

The truth is, even as a 56-year-old adult, I had to have the okay given by my "girl" Dr. (btw, that is not an official title; I have a GP whom I love but wasn't versed in gender affirming care, so my "girl" Dr. takes care of me for transition care); the surgeon; a letter from my therapist; a letter from a psychiatrist; and approval from insurance.

The final step was the insurance approval.

Everything was approved in early May, with the procedure scheduled for September. Of course, a monkey wrench was thrown into the gears when PRU (Poorly Run University) decided to fire me in late June, leading to my losing my insurance coverage on July 31. Since everything was already approved, I chose to go COBRA for a while so as not to delay the procedure.

Plus, I find childish glee in seeing that even though I am paying the full premium, "Poorly Run University" appears on my gender affirming surgery paperwork as the insurance group.

The day of the procedure is a bit of a blur.

I can say emphatically that I hated to go out without any makeup or jewelry, but otherwise the feeling was a combination of excitement and nervousness.

Excitement because of the day finally arriving, and nervousness just not knowing what to expect.

This was the first part of my transition that would not be reversible. I could stop taking hormones; change my name again; etc., but once the boys were gone, they'd be gone forever.

The last thing I remember before the operation is Dr. Surge coming to my cubicle.

She flung back the curtain and said, "Hey pretty girl, you ready for this?"

I burst into tears.

She came to my bedside, took my hand, and said, "Honey, I hope those are tears of joy."

I shared that they were, but also that I was just nervous. I have been fortunate in my life that I've always been a relatively healthy person. Other than being in the hospital having my tonsils removed when I was a kid, and my appendix removed when I was in my mid-twenties, I haven't been put under very often.

I felt terrible crying because I thought of the number of times she must perform this surgery, but it would often be under more dire circumstances—a man with cancer facing this would be devastated, and here I was wanting this but crying like a baby.

She held my hand and said, "You aren't going to believe how much better you're going to feel when this is over. I am so proud and happy that I get to do this for you. I promise you I am going to do an amazing job for you."

I said, "thank you."

She squeezed my hand, and that is the last thing I remember before I woke up.

I was told I would feel pain for a few days and was given a prescription for an opioid. They scare the hell out of me, so thus far I've just relied on Tylenol. I really haven't experienced pain—just some soreness.

My surgeon was right. I feel amazing.

I truly do.

I know people sometimes take issue with the term "gender affirming." I can tell you that "affirming" is the exact right word for this.

"So, what is different?"

The only part(s) of me that I considered "male" is gone.

My old friend "imposter syndrome" related to dysphoria is improved.

My underwear fits much better.

I get to cut down on the medications I take, as testosterone blockers are no longer necessary.

"Are there more surgical procedures in the future?"

As of now, the answer is no.

I have no idea what the future holds, but at present I am the happiest I have ever been in my life. I have amazing joy.

taco belle . . .

September 18, 2024

. . . it still feels strange . . . it still feels good . . .

Being flirted with and/or acknowledged as feminine by a man.

It happens somewhat regularly now—either a harmless flirt or maybe just a kind gesture.

A wink and smile, holding the door open, "let me get that for you, ma'am," "I like that scent you're wearing," etc.

Little things that can brighten a day.

On a recent stop at Taco Bell, I experienced the lesser-known-to-me "extended creepy older man flirting" encounter.

I ran in to get something quick for dinner. I always go in; the drive-thru is a nightmare, and I like using the order kiosk so I can make sure my order is correct.

I wasn't dressed particularly great—shorts and a t-shirt, hair in a messy bun, minimal make-up.

When I completed my order, I stood near the counter. There was an older man sitting at a table adjacent to the area where I was standing.

I heard him say, "You look really good today."

I turned around because I couldn't imagine he was addressing me. There wasn't anyone else around.

"Excuse me?"

He spoke in a gruff voice, "I was just saying how good you look today."

I said, "Thank you," and turned back around.

He then added, "But I know you look good every day."

I acted like I didn't hear him.

He then said, "I'm so tired, I've had a hard day."

I didn't acknowledge.

"My name is Barry."

I only turned halfway and just nodded my head. I pulled my phone out of my purse and started scrolling.

"What's your name?"

I didn't acknowledge.

"Now what's your name? I'm Barry."

Thank God for phones.

"DEANNA!" My order was ready, and the worker had called out my name. I crossed to get the bag.

"Deanna. A purdy name for a purdy girl!"

I just walked past him and made my exit.

Obviously, cis women have dealt with this kind of thing all their lives, but it creeps me out.

It is so conflicting for me.

It is very nice to be affirmed.

I always worry about it not being his intention to come off as creepy. Maybe he was just being nice and trying to be acknowledged by another human being.

If he'd been drop-dead handsome, would I have responded in the same way?

it went smoothly . . . not exactly . . .

October 5, 2024

This is an update on the surgical procedure I had 3.5 weeks ago. If you have no interest in such matters, please skip. Plenty of "the feels" in this one too.

Mentally and physically, I felt amazing after the orchiectomy. The first week came with some mild discomfort, swelling, and minor bleeding. Yes, I got to experience wearing a pad the whole time to keep things tidy—wings rock!

By the beginning of the second week, the bleeding had almost completely stopped, and other symptoms were ebbing. But on Sunday of that week, I noticed some additional bleeding. My two-week follow-up was scheduled for the following Tuesday with a nurse practitioner. While a bit surprised that there was still some bleeding, she wasn't overly concerned as there were no other issues. She advised me to just monitor it and call immediately if needed.

By the end of the week, the bleeding had mostly stopped except for a spot or two. I had a busy week at work—training sessions Monday and projects Tuesday and Thursday. Monday went smoothly, and I even skipped wearing a pad to bed, thinking I was safe.

Tuesday morning, I woke up to significant blood in my underwear. I didn't feel bad, and it appeared to have stopped. I went to work with no problems. By the time I got home, though, I was extremely tired. Being a "pretend patient" repeatedly can be surprisingly exhausting (I love it!). The surgical area was also sore, so I went to bed very early.

Wednesday, I decided to just rest. Spotty bleeding continued, and the soreness prompted me to call the nurse practitioner again. She couldn't see me that day, and I had a work project Thursday that couldn't be missed—students were already assigned, and there are usually no understudies. My appointment was set for Friday at 8 a.m.

Thursday went fine; I even got a flu shot at work. But by the end of the day, I was exhausted, and the surgical area was very tender.

At the Friday appointment, the nurse practitioner suspected a "bleeder" had been left behind, causing blood clots that could lead to infection—a rare but possible complication discussed pre-surgery. She left to contact Dr. Surge but returned shortly to inform me that the doctor was leaving town and headed to the airport. She suggested I start trying to arrange a ride as I might need emergency surgery; she then left me again to see if Dr. Surge had returned her call. I called my angel friend, and she was available to provide transportation if necessary. The nurse practitioner returned, she had spoken to Dr. Surge at the airport. Yes, I'd need to have surgery ASAP. Dr. Surge was now working on trying to locate a surgery team at one of the hospital affiliated surgery centers. If she couldn't locate one, I'd have to go to the Emergency Department on the main campus. I did not like this possibility.

Since Dr. Surge was at the airport ready to depart, I asked, "Who would be doing the surgery?"

"Dr. Surge will do it. She's changing her travel plans."

This amazing woman could have easily boarded her plane and sent me to the Emergency Department, but she didn't.

Fancy Nashville Surgery Center had a team ready. I'll spare you the saga of getting there. It's a bit of blur as the surrealness of sitting in a waiting room awaiting an orchiectomy is nothing compared to the whirlwind of being told:

"SURGERY NOW!"

Checking in at the Surgery Center, I felt a tug on the Halloween purse I was carrying. When I turned around, I saw the administrative assistant from where I work. We hugged as she complemented my purse. Her husband was there having a test done.

I was immediately called back for surgery prep.

When Dr. Surge walked into my cubicle, we both said, "I am so sorry!" I burst into tears.

"Why on earth would you be sorry?"

"Because I messed up your travel plans."

Dr. Surge squeezed my hand and said, "Are you kidding me? Do you think I'd let anybody other than me take care of you? I'm sorry this happened and I'm going to take care of it."

As the surgeon left the anesthesiologist came in to introduce himself. I was still drying tears.

"Are you okay?"

"I'm okay, I'm just nervous and a bit emotional."

He stepped over to me and placed his hand on mine and said, "**Ms.** Haynes, I want you to know that everyone here has one job: to look out for you. And I don't mind telling you we're great at our jobs." After the "feel-good cocktail," I don't remember a thing.

Waking up was slower than before, but there were no issues. Surgery was successful—cleaned out, repaired, and infection addressed. While getting dressed, the recovery nurse stayed in the room, turned her back, and let me work. I commented, "I look so terrible."

She turned, laughed, and said, "Honey, you look better than at least 95% of the women who walk out of here. Let me fix that hair of yours—it's a little flat in the back." She did.

I'm going to rest for a couple of days. Everything is fine as far as I know. "Recovery period" starts over.

I feel good this morning.

very funny doc . . .

October 11, 2024

Another surgery-related tale.

After my surprise surgery last Friday, I was told the surgeon had installed a drain because infection had started. It would only need to stay in for three days. I had an appointment scheduled with the nurse practitioner on Monday to have it removed.

When I got home Friday night, I saw the drain for the first time. Besides just being gross, I was a little shocked at another aspect of it.

Monday, at my appointment, the nurse practitioner asked if the drain had caused me any problems. I told her that physically it hadn't, but I certainly didn't appreciate Dr. Surge's sick sense of humor.

She looked confused. "What do you mean?"

"Well," I said, "with my surgery, I wasn't really expecting to have to add anything down there."

She smiled, still a little puzzled. I continued, "I just wasn't sure what to do with it. It seems a bit longer than necessary—maybe Dr. Surge was trying to be funny."

She lifted the sheet. A pause.

"Oh my... this REALLY is long."

"I told you!"

We both laughed out loud.

No issues. So far, I'm feeling great.

very excited . . .

October 16, 2024

I am really enjoying my new job. It's not only fun but also incredibly educational. I feel honored to play even a small part in the education of these future physicians.

Tomorrow is especially exciting because I'll be training on a case that deals specifically with a transgender/nonbinary patient. It's not only my first time doing this, but it's also the program's first time including such a case.

There's so much misinformation and misunderstanding about trans health issues. One of the biggest misconceptions is that seeking treatment is easy—it's not.

There are very few doctors in this state qualified to treat trans patients. Beyond the small numbers, the bigger problem is that when someone brave enough approaches a general practitioner for guidance, that doctor often doesn't know how to help. This isn't an insult; it's just a reality—they lack the training and knowledge to properly support trans and nonbinary folks.

The case I'll be working on is a simulation designed to assess whether someone carries cisgender or heteronormative biases when interacting with a trans/nonbinary patient seeking a PCP. Many people have never interacted with someone like me and may understandably feel unsure—or even nervous—about taking a basic medical history.

I'm so proud to be part of a program that is addressing this and excited to contribute to a more informed, compassionate future for healthcare.

mixed emotion . . .

October 23, 2024

I've been asked if I miss being at PRU.

The answer is simple: no, I do not.

That said, I do miss some true friends I had there, and I genuinely miss the students.

Earlier this week, I had the pleasure of having dinner with a former student. They are thriving and amazing, and it was wonderful to catch up with them.

During our conversation, they asked about my dismissal from PRU. I shared the abbreviated version—I don't wish to dwell on it.

Finally, my dinner companion said, "It makes me incredibly sad that you're not there anymore."

I was surprised and reminded them that they had told me on multiple occasions, "You need to get out of here."

They replied, "I am happy for you that you got out of there. But I was thinking that there is at least one student on that campus sitting in their dorm room right now who is just like me. The only difference is they don't have you to talk to. That makes me sad."

I don't know that I've ever felt such a mixture of happiness and sadness at the same time.

Representation and visibility are crucial. I am incredibly grateful and lucky to have so many amazing people in my life.

standardized trans . . .

October 25, 2024

I've completed the first trans/nonbinary project at work.

It went well—everyone involved seems pleased. The doctor who sponsored the project was incredibly kind. He was open and receptive to my comments and suggestions as we finalized the scenario. He also told me that everyone was very grateful to me for participating.

I shared that I was honored to be part of it. He responded, "I understand that, but I need you to know that we recognize how this requires you to put yourself out there in a way that most people wouldn't be comfortable with, and we are not only grateful but truly respect that."

I love this place.

The encounters went extremely well. The project was designed to identify prejudice and bias. To be honest, I didn't really expect much, as the students involved had chosen this as an elective. I assumed they would be sensitive and savvy enough to not go down that road.

The students were all super nice, though a few minor issues were identified—honestly, nothing major, just things many of us might say or do without thinking. Some assumptions were made without asking questions, mostly regarding my character's gender and/or sexual preference. (I am admittedly guilty of this too, as I was a little shocked when I met so many trans women who are lesbians.) A few awkwardly phrased questions here and there.

Bias and prejudice are often present even in those of us with the best intentions.

My favorite part of my job is giving face-to-face feedback to the students. I got to do that with this project, and they were all receptive to what I shared.

There was one thing I noticed during all the encounters. Honestly, I'm not sure if it was the students or my own insecurities—likely a bit of both—but I felt like Santa at a big department store when each student entered the exam room. That moment when a "child" sees the "big guy" in person for the first time. Santa... or a unicorn.

I didn't feel disrespected in any way. To be fair, the students weren't told in advance whom or what they would encounter, so understandably they were curious and maybe a little anxious about their "patient." Honestly, I'd probably run in terror if I entered the room and saw me sitting there!

I loved this project and the people involved so much. I am very proud.

hockey girl . . .

October 27, 2024

I attended my first Predators hockey game on Saturday night.

I attended, but I didn't actually watch the game. The Nashville Predators host various theme nights throughout the season. One series this year is "Music Heritage Night(s)," celebrating contributions from diverse groups in the Nashville community. Saturday was "Pride Music Heritage Night."

In addition to the music, the Preds invited various organizations to set up booths along the arena concourse. My Trans Support Group (TSG) was invited to participate, and I was honored to represent them.

I was a little apprehensive—not worried about safety or rudeness, but curious whether anyone would stop and engage with me. At a Pride event, you're surrounded by people celebrating diversity. A hockey crowd? That's different.

Our TSG Outreach Director was leading the group at Bowling Green Pride, so I handled the setup at Bridgestone. I arrived around 3:30 and got to work. The Preds staff were incredibly kind and welcoming. I was thanked multiple times for our participation, given a cool "Pred Head" pride t-shirt, and parking was validated.

Arena employees stopped by as they headed to their posts. We discovered a shared love of free candy! One young man asked for a piece. I said yes, and when he noticed our group's name—Trans Support Group—he froze mid-bite, eyes wide, mouth open.

He stammered, "Oh...are you...um...I mean...I don't want to be rude..."

"We may be a little past that," I said with a smile.

"Oh, I'm sorry, I didn't mean to..."

"It's okay! And yes, I am. I'd be happy to answer any questions you have."

He paused, nodded, and said, "I need to get to work now."

"Thanks for stopping by; have a good evening!"

I honestly don't mind interactions like that. Being a unicorn can be amusing sometimes.

As spectators filtered in, several people stopped to chat or grab stickers. Two cis couples asked if I would mind them asking questions.

I said, "Please do."

We had a really great conversation.

They asked things like:

"Is there a difference between a transvestite and a trans person?"

"What if you're unsure of a person's pronouns?"

"What is it like to be trans?"

They were genuinely curious, and I enjoyed answering. My friend JJ joined me, and we had a steady stream of folks engaging with us. Others would simply pass by and say:

"Y'all are beautiful!"

"I love y'all!"

"Thank y'all for being here!"

It was sweet and brought a smile to my face. Several cis attendees mentioned having a trans or questioning child or family member. Many LGBTQ+ community members were present too.

My favorite part was seeing young fathers encourage their sons to pick out inclusion-themed stickers—a simple gesture with a big impact.

As a people-watcher, I found it amusing how passersby would subtly look at our Trans Support Group sign, trying to see us without appearing obvious.

Eventually, the Outreach Director returned from Bowling Green for the last part of the event. As we began to break down the booth, a clearly inebriated male hockey fan repeatedly told us how "beautiful" we were. Each time he returned, he kept saying the same thing. On his final visit, he declared:

"I just gotta say it, you got balls. I mean it, you really got BALLS."

My response: "You wanna bet?"

Perfect ending.

I really appreciate the Preds organization for continuing their inclusion efforts, especially in an environment where such efforts are rare or discontinued. It was an amazing evening, and I'm so happy I got to be a part of it.

Oh, and by the way—the Preds won.

rant . . .

October 28, 2024

I've seen this meme posted several places and been sent it by a couple of sweet friends today.

It basically says if you don't know why your trans friend is scared then you're not really their friend.

To be honest, it pisses me off a bit.

I speak only for myself.

I am not scared.

I have never been less afraid/scared in my life about being who and what I am.

I fully recognize that I have lived most of my life with my share of white male privilege, and as a trans person I have been able to drag some of that privilege along with me. I also know that many of my trans brothers and sisters are not in the same circumstances that I am, and I do have concern for them.

My biggest fear, though, is for trans kids. Not only are they being denied critical medical care, but are under constant threat of bullying by peers and adults. They literally cannot use the bathroom at school without fear.

It is barbaric.

I also truly feel for the parents of these children. Many of the parents can't advocate for their child for fear of outing them and subjecting them to more ridicule and bullying. The parents also must consider the potential consequences for the rest of their family.

It is barbaric.

Anyone who would believe that a family with a trans child that seeks medical help would approach it flippantly is a moron.

I will not be scared.

I will represent.

I will be seen.

As far as the current political environment goes, I refuse to be afraid as a trans person. This isn't just about the trans community. I am afraid as a citizen of this country. Every single one of us should be.

Trans people are the current scary "boogie man," and being "anti-woke" is the call of the day. You only must look at history to see that an enemy is always needed to gain and build power.

That enemy will always need to get bigger and scarier.

It won't stop with trans people.

The definition of woke will continue to expand.

Open your eyes.

Those who don't learn from history are doomed to repeat it.

I received a message from a friend about the feelings I stated here. What follows is my response to what they had written:

October 29, 2024

There are obviously many people/things to fear in this world.

I did say in my post that I only speak for myself.

That remains the case.

In the last decade of his life, my dad would always beg me not to go shopping at the mall or go anywhere that many people were gathered. I was still presenting as male, so his fear for me was strictly based on the possibility and the likelihood, in his mind, of a mass shooter. I always went but eventually would not mention it to him until after the fact.

My intention in my post was not to present myself as some unafraid superhero taking on the world. I am far from that.

As I shared, my circumstances are different from a lot of my trans brothers and sisters.

For example, as a single trans person I don't have anyone that depends on me for anything. I have zero responsibilities to a partner, children or family. This allows me a great deal of freedom in a great many ways. One of those freedoms is not having to be concerned about what would happen to my loved ones if I found myself in a violent situation.

I believe there are some in our community that welcome and invite confrontation.

I do not.

That is not a judgement in any way on those folks; I admire and appreciate very much their commitment to the cause of inclusion and visibility.

I choose to focus on the positive and know that my outlook is often viewed as naive and Pollyanna-ish. This approach does not make me any better than anyone else, but I feel it is equally important and impactful.

It does not come without its own challenges. I have had many discussions with my therapist about my not wanting to be an "Uncle Tom/Aunt Joan" of the trans world and my concern about becoming a "token" at work.

You have mentioned before that you're not trying to fool anyone.

Neither am I.

If I ever pass, it is in no way my attempting to hide who or what I am. If I pass (there are times that I do), it is a result of my simply being me. It is not the result of some trick or performance.

I am **VERY** proud of being a trans person and I couldn't care less who knows it.

There is certainly more safety afforded to those who do pass.

You've heard me speak a lot about focusing on the joy.

My being "unafraid" has everything to do with my joy. I will not allow anyone or anything to rob me of that joy, and that includes fear. I am very appreciative that my circumstance allows me to take this approach.

Please know that I am very fearful of what we are potentially facing as a nation. That fear, in my opinion, is much bigger than just what the trans community might face.

I so admire you and the way you live your life. I love how alike and how different we are—that is equally important for people to see.

Much love my friend!

rant pt. 2 . . .

November 8, 2024

I shared my reaction last week to a meme suggesting that your "trans friends" are scared, and you should know why.

I basically stated that I refused to be scared but understood and empathized with any of my trans brothers and sisters that are frightened.

Then Tuesday's election happened.

I've been asked if I felt scared now that we are facing another four (?) years of the literal orange nightmare.

Please know that, as always, these are my own thoughts, and I am not suggesting that I speak for anyone else. I truly respect how others feel concerning the events of the past week, and I will always offer a sympathetic ear to anyone that needs it.

When he won in 2016, I was stunned. (This was long before I started transitioning or believed that it could become a reality for me prior to my being in at least my mid-sixties.) I got very depressed at the thought of what was going to happen to our country and stayed in that fog for well over a month. I had never been in that state over something political in my life. It was terrible.

Tuesday afternoon, I watched a little of the coverage. The reporters and pundits immediately gave me flashbacks to 2016, when they convinced me that Hillary would indeed win.

I turned off the coverage very quickly and decided then and there I wasn't going to get wrapped up in it the way I did back then. I didn't check back in on the coverage until about 8:30 Tuesday evening. He was racking up electoral college votes, and the pundits were discussing the "red mirage."

About that time, a friend texted to check in, and I replied with, "He is going to win; it's 2016 again."

He replied, "SHUT YOUR FACE!"

Excellent suggestion.

I turned off the coverage and watched a rerun of *Friends*. I then went to bed—I had a project Wednesday morning at work. This would not be 2016 again for me.

Following are my thoughts and takeaways from the results:

- I sincerely believe that there's not one thing anyone could have said or done that would have changed the outcome from Tuesday.

The blame game is pointless.

- I am grateful that his victory was decisive, so we don't have to endure years of the "they cheated" and "election interference" nonsense. The voters alone own this.

- Many in the LGBTQ community are legitimately terrified.

Will we suffer?

Absolutely.

But we are not the prize they are seeking; it is much bigger than those of us that make up less than 1% of the population.

- I believe the entire country is going to suffer the consequences of this election.

Do I want people to suffer?

Not as a general rule, but at this point, it must happen. The ONLY way some of these minds will be changed is if they are the victims of the policies that are coming our way.

They will be.

Often the only way to rebuild a house is to burn it down; I say, bring on the fire.

- The last time we had him as president with a Republican House and Senate, they couldn't get anything done except fight. These people cannot govern, and they have no desire to do so.

These power-hungry idiots will eat themselves up.

Many pundits say there is no way any of them will stand in his way this time—okay—see "let it burn" point.

- Health-wise, will he make it 4 years?

I have my doubts.

Yes, Mr. Eyeliner would be worse, but again, they'd eat themselves alive.

I will do my best to be brave. There will no doubt be days that I am down, depressed, tearful, angry, etc.

I am no martyr, but I am determined that I will not surrender my "joy" to anyone or anything.

I will not be silent.

I will continue to represent and try to make a difference the only way that I know how.

Will I pay some price for being who and what I am?

The odds are pretty good that I will.

Many have paid a much higher price for me to be able to live the life that I do.

Maybe it's my turn.

Regardless of what happens, I will face it with my **JOY** intact.

columbia house . . .

November 9, 2024

The *Wicked* movie will open soon. It looks amazing, and early reviews are very positive.

Around this time of year, when the 1939 film was traditionally shown on television, I almost always revisit a guilty pleasure from my childhood.

During the late seventies, the disco craze got arguably out of hand. What had been an amazing dance/music movement evolved into disco beaten into us at every opportunity.

There is, without a doubt, some amazing music from this period and some amazingly bad music.

We can all agree that *Disco Duck* was a bridge too far.

One of the trends to cash in was to reinterpret existing music with a disco beat.

Sweet compositions like the *Mork & Mindy* theme were re-orchestrated into the disco style. (I suppose I should admit that the disco *Mork & Mindy* theme has been my ringtone since Robin Williams passed.)

We suffered as the great Ethel Merman released a disco album of her Broadway standards—it is as wonderfully bad as you'd imagine.

Not all of the reinterpretations were bad, in my humble opinion. Occasionally, a legitimate musician would take on the task.

One of my favorites in this category was the musician Meco.

Meco is best known/remembered for his disco versions of the *Star Wars* and *The Empire Strikes Back* themes. They are honestly decent and certainly interesting listens.

My favorite Meco work is his lesser-known recording of the score from *The Wizard of Oz*, released in 1978.

I never knew it existed until my brother signed his soul over to Columbia House—twelve 8-track tapes for only a penny taped to a card.

I suppose when you must select twelve albums at once from a set list, you end up taking some chances. Needless to say, my brother did not care for his new acquisition of Meco's *The Wizard of Oz*.

His baby sister, however, LOVED it!

I listened to it any chance that I got.

I choreographed (*Waiting for Guffman* style) the entire album.

Even though the iTunes version doesn't have the track changes of my brother's 8-track copy I can still tell you where those breaks were when listening to it today. Naturally, I had to freeze during those "clicks" and pick my intricate dance moves back up when they were complete.

My brother used my love of this 8-track against me.

If he were mad at me or just having a bad day, he would take it away from me because it was "his" property.

Finally, the day came.

I have no memory of why he was upset with me, but still have a crystal-clear memory of his cowboy boot crushing the plastic of my beloved 8-track.

Tears running down my face, begging him not to do it.

His laughing at the destruction beneath his heel.

When he was satisfied that it was irreplaceably destroyed, he picked it up and handed it to me and said, "Oh you can have it, I don't want it anymore."

I looked for a new copy of the album, but was not successful, it was out of print. I never found a copy at yard sales or flea markets.

I did have a copy of the 45 single that was released so I didn't have to go cold turkey on it.

That Christmas, "Santa" delivered a copy of the Broadway cast album of *The Wiz*.

My "Santa" was always more of an "it's close enough" shopper.

I loved The *Wiz*, but it wasn't Meco.

Many years ago, I finally got a copy of the LP on eBay. Now it is available on iTunes.

short tale . . .

November 12, 2024

Yesterday I went to the grocery store.

I got to the door at the same time as a little old lady.

She was no more than 5' tall.

I motioned for her to go in first.

She stopped and said, "Go on and get yourself in there, shorty!"

It surprised me, and I laughed out loud.

I said, "Now I didn't make fun of you."

She replied, "Honey, I wasn't makin' fun of ya, I'm just jealous!"

milestone . . .

November 13, 2024

I reached another milestone in my gender-affirming care today.

Since beginning my hormone therapy, it has been achieved through estrogen patches.

I have been using two patches two times a week for some time now.

Insurance has covered them with a co-pay from me. They initially refused to cover the second patch when my dosage was upped. The clinical pharmacist at the gender clinic is a prince. He forced them to do so.

The patches are not uncomfortable, just a bit annoying. The adhesive does not like to come off, which is an asset in the shower or water, but a pain after the patch is removed and you're left with icky residue.

Even so, they have done their job admirably.

With my orchiectomy, my body was no longer capable of producing testosterone.

Hormone tests showed my testosterone level to be rock bottom after surgery. The truth is my testosterone number had been rock bottom even before the surgery.

What is surprising to most is that after the surgery, my estrogen level is what dropped significantly.

What the?!?

Our bodies and minds are so amazing. Those that believe everything must exist on a binary know nothing of science and nature.

Most of the testosterone I was producing since starting hormone therapy was being metabolized by my body into estrogen.

Since I no longer produce that T, my estrogen level dropped.

This wasn't a surprise; my doctor had explained it would happen.

Because of this, my two patches two times a week are no longer carrying the load.

Insurance will not pay for additional patches, and honestly, I don't want to deal with them either.

I have graduated to estrogen injections.

I know it sounds terrible to some, but honestly, one shot a week is not that big of a deal to me.

I'm excited to not have to wear my "scarlet letter/patch" any longer.

A bonus is insurance fully covers the injections.

I had my "orientation" and first shot today.

I am very happy.

you've done it . . .

November 19, 1024

Statistically speaking, we have all been in a public restroom at the same time as someone assigned the opposite sex of us at birth.

I have used the women's restroom in public situations for a year now.

I have somehow managed to not harass or bother anyone in the process.

The only thing that has been said to me thus far in these "women's spaces" is an occasional "Your hair is beautiful" or "I love your bag," or some variation of those kind comments.

If you are harassed in a public restroom, there are laws that exist that cover bad behavior, and you should report that person.

There is not one documented case of a trans person harassing anybody in a public restroom in this country.

There are more incidents reported of cis women being questioned about their presence in women's restrooms than trans women.

The earliest depictions of a "third sex" date to c. 7,000 BCE – c. 1700 BCE.

Seriously . . .

yesterday . . .

November 21, 2024

Yesterday was one of those days . . . one of those days that everything seems to go wrong or, at the least, doesn't go the way you anticipated.

I had a project scheduled at work.

This one was scheduled later in the day than usual and was a one-off (usually a sim is run back-to-back multiple times, but this one is scheduled for multiple days but only once each day). It was a new scenario, so we had trained a little more on it. I got to play a patient who had suffered a setback and is a bit of a bitch to an unsuspecting first-year resident.

The "bitch" roles are great fun to play and for some unknown reason seem to come easy to me.

I always do my best to get to campus early. You never know what Nashville traffic will throw at you, and I like having time to review the case when I get there.

Because the project was in the afternoon, I decided I'd give myself a little more time and grab lunch when I got there.

Lost in my music on the drive up, I got a scare when a rock hit my windshield. I was shocked and relieved to not see a crack in the glass.

A few minutes later, another noise startled me. I thought I had run over another rock and the wheel had caused it to hit underneath the car. I looked back but didn't see anything in the road in the rearview mirror.

I drove a minute or two more before it was obvious I had a flat tire.

I managed to make it to the shoulder of the interstate safely and got out to survey the damage.

I have a portable compressor that has saved me multiple times and had hopes that I could add enough air to get me to the next exit. I can change a tire (though I have yet to do it in a skirt and heels), but since my car is a hybrid, the space where a spare might be is filled with batteries.

The tire was absolutely destroyed.

I'm surprised that I didn't have more trouble getting off the road with the tire in such bad shape.

I had an hour and forty-five minutes before my work project started.

I called Honda Roadside, and they were kind but said it would be at least an hour before a tow truck would arrive. I got a text confirming; it said it would be ninety minutes.

I called my project supervisor. She was kind and gave me time to contact her to let her know if I was or wasn't going to make it.

I honestly had no hope.

I am still in disbelief that I made it to work and was only five minutes late from my call time.

The tow truck arrived within twenty minutes of my call . . . I know, right?

The driver was great. He got me and the car to a Honda dealership. The dealership arranged a car for me to get to work.

By the time I returned, my car was ready to go.

There were a million other little things that seemed to go wrong yesterday, i.e., a lost earring; a career-ending run in a brand-new pair of hose; etc.

The hose ended up in the trash. The earring reappeared in my bra at the end of the day. I'm always surprised by what I sometimes find in my bra.

The sim went well. When I was leaving work, my supervisor stopped me and said, "Dee, I watched your encounter."

Ugh . . . I was ready for notes.

"You do good work."

I admit that I needed that.

old friend . . .

December 4, 2024

I was in Walmart this morning looking at a clearance rack.

A Walmart employee came running up to me and said, "Girl, you are looking good! Your hair looks amazing, and that color is perfect for you!"

I had absolutely no idea who this woman was but replied, "Well, thank you; you're very sweet."

She sensed my hesitation and said, "You don't remember me, do you?"

"I'm sorry, but no, I don't."

"Ya do, I used to work at O'Charley's. I waited on you all the time!"

Ok, I was not who she thought I was, but just to be nice, I said, "Oh, okay, well it's good to see you and thank you!"

I started to walk away.

She calls after me in a loud voice, "Girl, you keep that hair color, it looks so good!"

"Thanks, have a great day."

Three takeaways:

1. It's always nice to be clocked as a girl.

2. It's always nice to get a compliment on the hair.

3. There is possibly another girl out there that looks like me . . . poor thing!

December 6, 2024

Some of my thoughts on the argument against Tennessee's ban on hormone blockers for trans kids.

I am certainly no expert on the subject, but I get so tired of the constant purposeful misrepresentations of these issues.

The law, which is clearly written with sexual bias, only bans these treatments for trans kids. Cis kids are not affected by the ban and continue to be prescribed these medications if parents and doctors decide they are needed.

Every drug/prescription you, I, or anyone else takes comes with potential risk. We assume those risks when we take the medication.

In all other cases, if the child is under eighteen, a parent is allowed to consent for the child.

Our state legislature has assumed this responsibility for trans children regardless of parent or medical professional input. They claim their interference is all an effort to "protect the children," as if these people give a damn about the trans kids that brought the case.

It is my understanding that puberty blockers are not allowed to be prescribed for any child for more than twenty-four months to prevent the risk of irreversible changes.

There is no surgery involved in the prescription of puberty blockers. To conflate this treatment with surgery is ignorant.

A trans child has never been prescribed puberty blockers without the consent of the child, a parent, and multiple medical professionals.

The constant misinformation that any gender-affirming medical intervention—no matter the patient's age—is easy without thoroughly vetted medical diagnosis is infuriating.

I feel so much for the parents of these kids who only want to help and do what is right for their child.

Legislature knows best.

When I was born, upon advice of a doctor and my parents' consent, I was given a circumcision. My penis was irreversibly altered—some would say mutilated—without my consent.

The legislature seems to have no issues with this irreversible, nonconsensual procedure.

Just like all surgeries, treatments, and medications, circumcision comes with potential risks. No need to "protect the children" in this instance, though.

Why should any of this concern you or me?

The desire to ban trans medical care will not stop with minors; adult treatments will no doubt be on the agenda soon.

Supreme Court Justice Frat Boy suggested that the same reasoning that did away with Roe v. Wade should be applied in this case.

If that is our new standard, it can and will be used in many cases. No one can be so naive as to believe this isn't the beginning of systematically stripping away more personal freedoms.

It may not be your freedom at risk today, but are you so confident it won't be tomorrow?

dr. mrs. garrett . . .

December 13, 2024

I've shared before that one of my concerns before I began transition was that my life would be a constant hellscape of being mistreated and ridiculed.

I think many cis people have the same thoughts about what a trans person experiences.

I often end an online post with "I am very lucky."

I am.

So far, I have not had many negative encounters. The ones I've had have been minor.

Not all my trans brothers and sisters have that same journey in their daily lives.

I don't share much of the "negative" because they seem so insignificant and honestly pale in comparison to the joyfulness that I've experienced.

Friends have asked about any negatives, so I thought I would share one. (Again, I stress that I am very lucky, and in the great scheme of things, this was certainly a minor blip.)

I was misgendered.

Yes, it happens.

I don't let being called "sir" or "him" bother me if it is an innocent thing. We all make mistakes. I have cis female friends that get misgendered more often than I do.

For me, it comes down to intention—if it is done purposefully, then I do have a problem with it happening.

This situation happened at work months ago, shortly after I started my new job.

If you don't know, I work at BTMC as a standardized patient ("acting" patients used to give students a "real" experience). Throughout the application and audition process, I was very open about being a trans person. I never try to "hide" who and what I am.

I also don't feel the need to wear a sign around my neck—like most of my trans brothers and sisters, I just want to live my life the best that I can.

I felt (and still do) that the work environment was a very welcoming and safe space.

Most of the scenarios we simulate are written as binary (male/female). The diagnoses in the simulations are usually secondary to the students having live interaction with a human patient. There are a few projects that do require the "patient" to be either male or female, but again, they are relatively rare.

I have not had an issue with any of the students accepting my feminine presentation. I usually never know if they know or suspect that I'm trans or just accept what I'm presenting.

On a couple of occasions, I have had a queer student that entered the room, looked at me, and revealed a very broad smile on their face. It can't be said enough—representation is important.

There have been a couple of times I've spoken with the preceptor (doctor) on a project and revealed that I was trans. Usually, they share that they "had no idea." It's such a tricky thing because it doesn't and shouldn't matter, but I admit I am always curious if they can clock me.

Only once has there been a project where a doctor intentionally clocked me with "he" and "him" during the sim.

The project I was working on involved first-year/first-semester medical students. It would be the learners' first time encountering a "real" patient. The students worked in teams of two and entered the exam room together with a preceptor.

The students would enter, take a patient history, and take my blood pressure. My patient history was as a cisgendered married female. Although I was clad in a hospital gown, I did have hair, make-up, jewelry, and answered all of their questions as a married woman.

The students had no training at taking a blood pressure, so the doctor was required to assist them.

The first day there were no issues.

A couple of the students asked me my preferred pronouns when they entered. All addressed me as Mrs. and/or the correct feminine pronoun.

Well, there was an issue with the blood pressure taking. The students were nervous and more than once they pumped the cuff too tight.

It was cute and humorous.

The second day I was assigned to the same examination room. The preceptor on observation duty was different.

I try not to prejudge people, but I couldn't help but notice this doctor's hair.

I was fascinated at the architecture of it. Her style is what I call "Mrs. Garrett" hair. Mrs. Garrett ("Girls. Girls! GIRLS!") from *The Facts of Life* had a huge bun atop her head. Usually, when you see someone today with this hairstyle it is associated with fundamentalist Christians. No judgment, but I thought, "Wow, how unusual for a doctor to have such a complicated hairdo." Most medical professionals seem to opt for a lower-maintenance coiffure.

The first encounter began—the students entered the room with the doctor. The students were sweet and took the medical history with no problems.

Then the blood pressure check.

The doctor announced to the students, "**HE** is going to need to be on the exam table for the blood pressure check."

Did she just say, "He?"

Maybe I just didn't hear it correctly.

Dr. Mrs. Garrett then pulled the blood pressure cuff off the wall and said, "**HE** is going to need a bigger cuff."

Two things:

One. She definitely said "He." I thought this was a bit strange, but maybe she was asking the male student to get the bigger cuff from the cabinet.

Two. I was in the same exam room as the day before. The exact cuff that she wanted replaced with a bigger one had taken my blood pressure eight times the day before.

Did this bitch just call me fat?

From that point on, it was obvious that she was addressing me as "**HE** this," "**HE** that," "**HE** needs" . . . in an endless stream.

I did not say anything.

The simulation was still going on, and we are expected not to break character.

I was shocked at her behavior but did not feel comfortable calling the doctor out in front of the students.

I didn't say anything.

On most of the projects, we are asked to give feedback.

Most often, feedback is given by means of a computer survey form. On this project, we were asked to leave the exam room. The doctor would then speak to the students about the encounter. Finally, the SP would reenter and give feedback in person.

When I left the exam room, I felt stunned.

I was just surprised and disappointed that it had happened here. If one of the students had made a mistake, I would not have thought anything about it, but this was very intentional.

Intentional and continual.

As I was putting my thoughts/comments together, I decided my job was to respond to the students. I would just let her behavior go.

I got the signal to return to the exam room to share my feedback.

On the short walk down the hallway, I had a single thought: "Fuck that bitch."

I walked in and sat down facing the two students and Dr. Mrs. Garrett.

I had a smile on my face and said in a sweet voice, "I just want the three of you to know that if you ever find yourself in a situation with someone and you are not sure of how they identify or what pronouns they prefer, you should always ask before making an assumption. It's perfectly acceptable to not know or be sure, but . . ." I turned and looked directly at Dr. Mrs. Garrett and continued, "it is disrespectful and unprofessional if you choose to make an assumption with zero consideration for the person you are addressing."

I turned back to the students and shared my feedback with them.

I had Dr. Mrs. Garrett the next round too. She did not address me in any way the second time.

Project days are a bit chaotic, and I don't always see my supervisor other than in passing.

The next day, I got an email from her telling me I had done a good job.

I responded, "Thank you," and added that I had something that I would like to speak to her in person or on the phone about.

She immediately responded that she was available to speak on the phone then.

I called and explained to her what had happened. I emphasized that I wasn't upset or officially complaining, but I wanted to make her aware of what had happened in case something was said.

I also wanted to make sure she was okay with how I handled it.

She apologized that it had happened and thanked me for the way I handled it.

She added that any situation that gave me an opportunity to advocate, she expected me to take it.

All was good.

The next day, I got another email from her.

She forwarded an email she got from the doctor that oversaw all the students involved in the project.

The two students who were in my encounter had visited his office. They shared that they were embarrassed and concerned that they had "disrespected" me. They wanted to apologize to me.

My supervisor informed him that I had spoken to her about the situation and that she had watched the encounter (every encounter is recorded and archived) and was disappointed by the doctor's behavior.

They agreed to meet and discuss how to avoid future issues.

I let my supervisor know that I didn't feel the students had done anything wrong and that I certainly appreciated their apology. I did not feel they owed me one.

It was certainly a wonderful gesture on their part.

magic changes . . .

December 22, 2024

I finally got around to reading *Grease: Tell Me More; Tell Me More* which is about the original Broadway production of *Grease*.

This show (and film) has always had a special place in my heart.

Grease was the first musical I saw live on stage and that coupled with the film, helped shape my love of the theatre.

Many people in theatre look down on the show.

It's considered a "slight" musical and (rightly) way overdone. It is one of those shows that has developed a "schlock" reputation, though it had a major impact on musical theatre history.

It fascinates me how the show itself has become completely sanitized over the years.

The original production's humor was decidedly "blue," and the creators believed the characters in the show were not likable. They saw them as the kids that most people avoided and feared in high school.

I have always thought the show was just pure fun, and over my career I've gotten to design it three times and direct it once.

Wait a tick, aren't your posts usually about your transition experiences at this point?

There is a bit of connection to my transition story . . .

The score has one of my favorite show tunes; "Those Magic Changes." I got the chance to sing it on stage once in a showcase.

In the show, "Those Magic Changes" is sung by the character "Doody."

Fun fact: Years before the film, John Travolta was cast in the first national tour of the show as "Doody." In the film, he sings a bit of the song to Sandy at the dance.

In my twenties, my then best friend and I spent a lot of time talking about shows and playing the "who'd you play in . . ." game.

They were a bit surprised when *Grease* was the subject, and I said though I was confident I would be cast as "Roger," I would want to play "Doody."

Yes, my true preference would have been "Rizzo."

They laughed and said, "No one has ever said they want to be Doody!"

We speculated on how someone might acquire such a nickname. None of the scenarios we considered were particularly flattering to poor "Doody."

After that conversation, my friend started calling me "Doody."

Exclusively.

I didn't particularly mind, although in some public/social situations I got some strange looks.

After a couple of months, my friend started shortening the name "Doody" to just "D."

Although it didn't influence the choice of Deanna as my name, decades before I started my own "Magic Changes" (HA!), I was already answering to my destined name, D(ee).

another tall one . . .

December 23, 2024

I was shopping this morning.

I heard a female voice from behind me call out, "Hey there tall lady!"

I turned around and had to look up to see the face of a woman several inches taller than me.

She had a huge smile on her face.

Looking up to her I said, "Hey there yourself! I think you win this round."

She laughed and said, "I'd prefer we call it a draw."

I replied, "I can live with that."

"Have a great day; Merry Christmas!"

oh brother . . . pt. 1 . . .

January 2, 2025

I've shared about my parents and my relationship with them as a child. I haven't written much about my brothers.

To say my relationship with my siblings was strained, frustrating, and complicated would be a massive understatement.

I always struggled with how differently I was treated in the family dynamic. I guess all kids have those moments where they are convinced that they had to be adopted; this would have explained so much.

The truth is I have come to accept that I was indeed the daughter/sister in the family, though at the time none of us were consciously aware of it.

I'm certain that my being the youngest added another layer to our warped dynamic.

My brothers were Tommy (Thomas Earl) and David (David Wayne).

We were born three years apart in November. Pretty awesome family planning for the 1960s. I always say we know what my parents were doing on Valentine's Day in '61, '64 & '67. (And one dark day in the early 70's when I walked in their bedroom . . . eek!)

Several years before my mother passed, I bought one of those prompt books (*Conversations with My Mother*) to interview and preserve some family history. She refused to let me interview her but instead filled the book out herself (in less than twenty-four hours).

One question included was: "What is each child's greatest strength?"

Both my brothers had passed at this point, and this is what she wrote about them:

Tommy: Loving – meeting new people AND learning to use them.

David: Being difficult.

She also added in another response that one of her biggest surprises with her children was they were all completely different. She wrote that we "never seemed to belong together as a group."

Her responses really surprised me in their truth. Throughout my life, particularly after their passing, her tendency was to deify my brothers.

Please know that it isn't my intention to speak ill of the dead. This is simply my attempt at telling and understanding my story.

For Pt. 1, I will focus on my middle brother, David.

My older brother, Tommy, will be a much more complicated and painful story to share in the future Pt.2.

I was conceived to be a girl.

I have no idea if that was ever shared with my older siblings and if they were anticipating a baby sister with my arrival.

My mother had a difficult time with her pregnancy with me and had to be on bed rest for a significant amount of time.

I don't know if these two things affected my relationship with either of my brothers.

I've often wondered if they, like I suspect my mother, somehow subconsciously knew I was a girl.

It is more likely that Tommy might have known that about me, as David never knew or wanted to know anything about me.

David did not like me.

I guess I should clarify and say David never gave any indication to me that he liked me or ever cared anything about me.

This is not a "poor pitiful me" line, it is just the truth.

I clarified my statement because as I reached high school and my adult years, I would have friends of his share with me that he did talk about me. He'd apparently tell his friends that he was proud of me, how smart I was, how talented I was.

Like my mother, he NEVER gave any indication to me that he felt or thought those things. In fact, it was always the opposite.

My mother always said he was just like her mother.

My maternal grandmother, Mama Berta (we were not allowed to call her granny), was without a doubt one of the most miserable people you could ever meet. I don't say that with any satisfaction.

She was, in a word, horrible.

She lost her husband early; had a daughter she never wanted (my mom); was epileptic; obviously bi-polar (not diagnosed); and a prescription drug addict.

She never set foot in our house after I was born because it was "too crowded" with my addition.

In the six or seven years that I knew her, she never hung a Christmas decoration; never gave a gift (birthday or Christmas); never baked a cookie or offered a snack; never gave a kiss, hug, or smile; or anything else you'd think a grandmother might enjoy doing.

Again, I stress that these aren't complaints, just facts.

One story my mom always shared about her mother happened after her dad had passed away.

My mother was very lucky to have had the grandparents she did; both maternal and paternal grandparents were amazing and helped my mother survive childhood.

Mom's paternal grandparents were as supportive as possible when my grandfather passed, even though Mama Berta was horrible to them.

One night, after an argument, my mother's uncle had enough of her and punched her lights out. Of course, I nor anyone in the family would condone violence, but apparently the consensus was "she had it coming."

There was no physical damage, but when she came to, she had amnesia.

She was admitted to the hospital and stayed for multiple days. Again, there was a consensus from family and medical staff that she was faking the amnesia.

My mother hadn't been allowed to visit her but finally the doctor thought it might help.

My mother's maternal grandmother (who everyone called "Lou" –no one in my mom's family wanted to be called granny it seems) who was a saint of a woman, took my mother "to town" and let her pick out a new dress before the planned visit.

Mom was proud of the dress she picked and wore it out of the store to the hospital.

When she walked into her mother's room, her mom took one look at her and said, "Betty, that is the ugliest goddamn dress I've ever seen!"

My mother was crushed, but miraculously the dress was so ugly that the amnesia was instantly cured.

As terrible as the woman was, there was something I admired about her.

She was rumored to have had an illegal abortion before she married. I don't know any details other than the entire town knew the rumor.

Then in the 1960s, she moved in with a man and spent the rest of her life "shacked up" (that's what my mom called it) out of wedlock.

I have mentioned that she was terrible, but she was also a badass woman who didn't "give a spit" about what the world thought.

I greatly admire that about her.

My mother was correct when she'd say, "there is absolutely nothing you can do to please her." If you dared show any happiness or joy around her, you'd better believe she was going to end it.

My brother David was very much like her . . . at least with his immediate family.

David had a lot of friends, and he was the hilarious life of the party with them. Fun loving, sweet, generous to all those around him.

He had fans at all his favorite hangouts. Those of you from Columbia will recognize them: The Pizza Maker; Shooters; The By-Pass Deli.

In those places, my brother was a redneck version of "Norm" from *Cheers*.

If you knew my brother as a friend, I think you were very lucky.

With family, though, he was a terror.

My parents let him get away with so much crap, I suppose in the hopes that he wouldn't throw one of his infamous tantrums.

He would always give a valiant try to ruin any good time at hand: holidays, birthdays, vacations, etc.

To me, he was a nightmare.

Although we initially shared a bedroom, we did nothing together.

I wasn't even permitted to look at any of his toys, much less touch them.

I'm not sure we could have been any more separate than we were. I learned at a very young age not to engage with him.

For me, it just wasn't worth the effort.

He always complained that because I was the youngest, I "got whatever I wanted."

I did have a lot of things, but he conveniently ignored the fact that it was because I paid for them.

My needs were very much provided by my parents.

"Needs" were one thing, but "frivolous" spending was another.

I wanted an Atari 2600. NO WAY were my parents going to shell out that much money for a game. However, my mother would take me to Rose's Department Store and teach me how to put one on layaway; how much I'd have to pay each week to get it out, and the consequences if I missed payments.

The first VCR in our house wasn't on the family TV in our den. It was in my bedroom. Because I wanted it, put it on layaway, and got it.

My bedroom was also equipped with HBO and Cinemax—luxuries in the 1980s. If I paid the bill and kept my grades up, my parents didn't care.

Yes, it would have been nice to be a spoiled child, but I am always grateful that I was taught how to get things at such an early age.

Both my brothers could have done the same thing but never had the interest or patience to pay something off.

It was much easier for David to create the story that I was given all of these things and he was ignored.

David struggled with a physical challenge as a child.

To be honest, I'm not sure exactly what the diagnosis was, but for a period during childhood, he had to wear leg braces and "special" shoes from a store in downtown Nashville. It certainly wasn't polio, and he overcame whatever it was in time.

He became the only athlete out of the three of us.

I think because of this, he was always more spoiled than Tommy or me. He remained spoiled until his death.

I know you're thinking, "Now Dee, that's just sour grapes."

Wrong.

As adults, when I would point out to my parents that they were doing things for him that he should be doing himself, they'd insist that I was jealous.

My response was always, "Yes, yes I am."

Just some examples of the things my parents would do for him up until he passed away in his forties:

My brother never once bought a stick of deodorant. My mother always provided this for him.

My brother never once bought a roll of toilet paper. Again, provided by my mother.

The list of items provided by my mother included all toiletries. He had his own fully stocked cabinet at her house where he could come and take any supplies he needed for his apartment.

Mom always made sure his truck insurance was paid. He would sometimes make payments of $25 a week to go toward her payments.

Never bought a vehicle without my parents cosigning the note. If he missed a payment, they would cover it at the bank.

Never got his oil changed. My dad would keep up with it and tell him, "I need to take your truck tomorrow to get the oil changed." This would almost always end in an argument, with the result being my brother telling Dad when he would permit him to take the truck in for an oil change.

Please know I am not saying my mom never helped me out financially—in my younger years she certainly did. She was always my "last resort," and they were true financial transactions.

Another way that I was different was my mother could tell you exactly how much she spent on me every year. She kept a little spiral memo book in her purse and wrote down whenever she spent money on me. Food, clothing, etc. were all written down, and she could pull out the running total at any time.

She never did this with my brothers.

I now tell myself she just wanted to ensure her daughter knew how to be financially independent.

Years after Tommy had passed away, my parents' fiftieth wedding anniversary was approaching. I wanted to give them a reception. My mother was excited about it and asked that I include David. I told her that I would, but I was confident it wouldn't end well.

When I spoke to him, he said he'd help but he "wasn't payin' for nothin'."

Shocking.

I attempted to include him time and time again:

No response to different cake pictures.

No response to whom we should ask to help serve.

No response to the invitation that had to go to the printer.

When he found out I had sent the invitation to the printer without his approval, he exploded.

He knew I was "only doing this to make yourself look like a big man!" (I promise I never in my life have wanted to look like a big man.) He ranted to me and our parents that he would no longer offer any assistance.

I could live with that.

He didn't show up for the reception. This truly hurt my parents and placed a cloud over the whole affair.

I could go on with countless stories like this but will spare you.

The truth is my mother desperately needed to be needed, and both my older siblings obliged her need.

Her daughter did not.

David was an alcoholic.

To my knowledge, his drinking never caused problems with his employment.

Throughout my life, I pleaded with my mother to take her name off his truck title and insurance, as I was terrified he'd end up hurting someone on the road.

David wasn't a mean drunk but a crying "I love you!" drunk.

If he ever was drunk and said, "I love you!" he would be ten times more of an ass to you the following days.

It is sad to admit, but for most of my life I avoided him as much as possible.

A couple of years before his death, he had a health scare related to his alcoholism.

It appeared that he was successful in his sobriety in his final years. Unfortunately, it had no effect on the way he and I interacted.

In the end, I didn't really know my brother, and he didn't know me.

I wish that weren't true.

I always think about if I had been a cis girl at birth how the family dynamic might have been different.

Would he have been a protective big brother or still filled with rage and resentment toward me and the rest of the family?

I suppose it's pessimistic, but my belief is it would ultimately have made our relationships worse.

There is no doubt that my dad would have doted on his baby girl, but I'm confident the issues Mom and I had would have been significantly amplified.

I don't believe for a minute it would have changed anything about my relationship with my brothers.

I sometimes hear some trans brothers and sisters lament about how they regret not having those teenage years as their authentic selves.

I understand that completely, but I don't regret that at all.

I believe things work out how they're supposed to work out.

I am convinced that had I been a girl in my teen years, I'd have ended up pregnant and forced into a marriage with someone with no real love.

Instead, I got Stephen, who kept me safe and led me to the life I can lead now.

I am grateful.

slumber party . . .

Most people don't enjoy going to the doctor.

When you go to the doctor, you generally are not happy about it. You have an ailment and, as a last resort, you make an appointment seeking help to resolve it.

Those that are transitioning are also seeking relief from an ailment. Their gender care doctor is, in many ways, their savior. They literally help transform trans people's lives for the better.

These medical professionals save lives.

Trans patients generally feel very close to and protective of their doctor.

I have never dreaded an appointment with Dr. Estra (my gender care doctor, aka my girl doctor).

Many months ago, at a Trans Support Group meeting, a trans woman shared that she was ready to start hormone therapy and asked the group for recommendations for a doctor to assist her.

There were certainly recommendations.

There aren't that many options when seeking a physician that specializes in trans care, but the discussion about these three or four physicians in the Nashville area went on for some time.

Many members shared the amazing things about their physician and why their doctor was the one to see.

I didn't participate in the debate even though my own physician, Dr. Estra, was included in the glowing testimonials.

The discourse continued for some time.

The woman who had asked the original question, in an attempt to move on, said multiple times, "Thank you so much, you've certainly given me some good names to consider."

I loved how the topic seemed to evolve into a "my dad can beat your dad up" dynamic.

Nurses and other office staff became part of the battle-of-the-docs throwdown.

Finally, the "thanks for the suggestions" statement was offered again.

It did the trick this time, and the room fell silent.

I raised my voice and said, "I am sure all these doctors are great. There is one thing that hasn't been mentioned that you might really want to consider. Dr. Estra is *really* cute."

Suddenly I felt like I was at what I'd imagined a teenage slumber party to be like.

Laughter and squeals.

"Yes!"

"He is!"

"So adorable" broke out.

I love the passion of trans folk!

Naturally, I shared this story with Dr. Estra at my next appointment.

He laughed but was obviously a bit embarrassed at hearing it.

You'll be shocked to hear that this made him even more cute.

oh brother . . . pt.2 . . .

January 5, 2025

WARNING: *This post discusses sexual abuse. Please read at your own discretion.*

My relationship with my oldest brother, Tommy, was the opposite of the one I had with David.

At least, it started that way.

As a friend of mine would say about her first-born brother: Tommy was born in a manger. He was the golden boy—the smartest, the most handsome, the most charismatic of all of us.

My mother was enamored with him. I don't think that's unusual for a mother and her first-born son. I don't really remember my father being particularly close to Tommy. Tommy always had an air of thinking he was a little better than those around him. My dad would always say to him, "Don't get above your raisin', son." Tommy hated when he heard that and usually took it as a challenge. Even with that separation, there was a level of respect between the two of them.

David and Tommy didn't appear to be close either. Just like with Dad, there seemed to be an understanding between them. They didn't have many interests in common. It always felt to me that Tommy was aware of David's sullen behavior but, unlike the rest of us, he didn't engage it or let it bother him in the least. He was above it.

Growing up, there were many times my dad would take Tommy and David to do things—boy things—a stock car race, a basketball game, a trip to the state fair, etc. I would always ask to go on these excursions but would be told I was too young. I would have to stay home with my mother. I have no idea if this was a subconscious separating of me as "not a boy" or maybe "not boy enough."

Staying at home with Mom while the boys were out was not necessarily a girl's night for me. We might go out to eat or do a little shopping, but it was basically a night off for her while I did my own thing.

I distinctly remember one time I was left out of boys' night but didn't ask to go because it was the night the final episode of *The Mary Tyler Moore Show* was going to air. I was nine years old and very excited to watch.

I idolized my big brother.

Compared to my interactions with David, I was the opposite with Tommy. He and I shared a love of movies and television. He made a real effort to be kind to me and include me in a lot of his activities.

My earliest memories of us doing things as brothers were Sunday afternoons. Sundays were always church and then lunch at my granny's house (Dad's mother was an absolute "granny"). It feels like most Sundays we would ask my mother if we could go to see a movie after lunch. We'd be dropped off at the Polk Theatre to watch a Sunday afternoon matinee. David rarely joined us, and if he did, he never sat with us.

I loved going to the movies with my big brother.

As a child, I honestly felt that Tommy was the one member of the household that genuinely liked me.

David and I shared a bedroom. Tommy, as the oldest, had his own. He had a full-size bed, a television, and a stereo in his room. He was fine with me being in his room if I wanted to listen to his records or tapes or watch his TV when he was at work. (Tommy started working at a neighborhood market when he was thirteen or fourteen.)

When Dad and David were watching a sports event, or Mom had to watch something boring like *Barnaby Jones* or *Cannon*, Tommy and I would lie on his bed watching something cool or listening to music.

What I am about to share is difficult. There are specifics I will not share, and there are some details I have no memory of at all.

When I was around the age of nine or ten (Tommy would have been fifteen or sixteen), he started touching me in places he shouldn't have when I spent time in his room.

It became a regular occurrence and escalated quickly.

It was a regular game of how quiet we could be, listening in case we heard footsteps approaching. The "you can't tell anybody" discussions were had.

There is a part of sexual abuse that is not spoken of often. It is the worst part for many survivors. It is why shame and guilt can smother the victim.

This is not easy.

The truth is I loved my brother. This person I loved was telling me what he was doing was what was supposed to happen—"it's natural." I was "special, and it's just between us."

This is where it really gets messed up: someone I loved was touching me sexually, and the truth is—it felt good. The thought that something was wrong about it was not in my mind. The shame and guilt about this are still horrendous.

Did this in any way lead to me being a trans person?

Hours of therapy have been devoted to that question. The answer is no. Examples of my dysphoria predate the abuse. The only way it relates to my trans-ness is that it offered another example of my dysphoria.

This too is hard.

As what he would do to me progressed, I started wrapping his bedspread around my body. The first time I did it, he asked what I was doing, and my reply was, "Girls wear dresses." From that point on I always created my "dress," but he never mentioned it again. It was just something that I did. Any therapists or psychiatrists I've spoken to about it seem to agree that it was my way of getting to a safe place; the bedspread became my own "secret garden."

Around ten or eleven years old, I was offered a job at the same market where he worked. Once I started working, the abuse stopped. I found out later that he tried every way in the world to get the owner not to hire me.

When he stopped allowing me to be in his room with him to watch television, I was deeply hurt. I did not understand. This person I loved was suddenly mean and cruel to me. (If you read my MECO entry, it happened during this period.)

Sometime, somehow, the memory of what had happened repressed in my mind. I reached a point where I never thought about it any longer.

Tommy started dating regularly. We eventually became friends again. He still felt like my only real ally in the house. He even occasionally asked me to go on dates with him and his girlfriend.

He started college but dropped out to get married. This was the beginning of a complete breakdown and the self-destruction of his life.

When I finally moved out of our house to attend college at Austin Peay, the memories of abuse began to emerge. I started having nightmares and flashbacks. When I moved to Clarksville, my mom had insisted that I come home every weekend. With the memories invading my mind, I started staying at school on the weekends. On a visit that I couldn't avoid, my mother confronted me about no longer wanting to come home. I had no intention of ever speaking to her about what had happened, but I finally blurted it out.

She slapped me and called me a liar.

She eventually confronted Tommy about it. He told her he had merely taught me how to masturbate.

She confronted me again and laid into me, saying I shouldn't spread rumors when "boys will be boys." She told me I should be thankful that he had taught me about masturbation, and that he was doing what big brothers were supposed to do. I told her that if that was what she needed to believe, that was fine.

Later that night she returned to me and offered, "*IF* it happened... *IF* it happened, I am sorry." My mother and I never discussed it again.

About five years later, during one of Tommy's many recovery attempts, I was invited to participate in one of his therapy sessions. I declined. My mother asked, pleaded, begged, and demanded that I do so. I relented. During the session with his therapist, he admitted the extent of what he had done to me. He said he was "sorry." His therapist then demanded that I forgive him. I thanked him for admitting what he had done and said that was all I had to say.

My brother's life after he quit college could easily be described as a train wreck. Here are just a few highlights of his self-destruction:

His marriage lasted about a year. His drinking got out of hand and he ended up in a rehab program.

He married a second time, which again lasted about a year.

After his second marriage failed, he announced he was gay.

He became a self-described "slut," and serious drug use joined his drinking habit. He was in and out of rehab programs multiple times.

He was banned from every department store in Nashville for shoplifting.

He eventually decided to move to Kansas City. When I asked him why he was moving, his answer was, "To get AIDS."

When he returned, he was HIV+ (he never developed AIDS) and shooting cocaine.

He moved back to my parents' house multiple times. The final time he lived with them ended with him physically attacking my dad and leaving a hole in their living room wall where he missed my dad's head with a punch.

He stole money and jewelry from my parents.

He forged many checks.

He lied about anything and everything.

I was always amazed at the power he had over people. He could go out any day of the week and get a job. Even when he screwed people over, they loved him.

At one point, he was a night auditor for a motel in Nashville. Part of his payment was that he got to live in a room at the motel. As the night auditor, he was there alone. One night he decided he wanted to go party. He took half—seriously, half—of the cash from the drawer and walked out of the motel office, leaving it unattended and unlocked. The owner didn't press charges and even allowed my dad to come by and get all of Tommy's belongings from the room he'd been staying in for six weeks.

I initially tried to be supportive but reached a point where I was done. I was not going to be hurt by him anymore, and so I cut him out of my life for good.

Mom and Dad blamed me and said I was being cruel and unforgiving. I can't tell you the number of times Dad told me I "should be ashamed of myself" for how I treated my own brother. (To my knowledge, Dad never knew what Tommy had done to me, though I think he still would have thought I shouldn't have cut him out of my life.) My parents believed it was my way of punishing him, but the truth is it was a way for me to survive.

Once I made that decision, I never spoke to him again. He never made any effort to contact me.

When he reached his forties, he had settled down a bit. He had a full-time partner that he lived with in Florida. His partner had a decent job with a county government but lost it when it was discovered that he and Tommy were using the county's fuel dispensary to fill their personal cars. Both the partner and Tommy started to spiral again.

Six months later, Tommy was in hospice with cirrhosis of the liver.

I'm not proud of it, but the only thing I really felt at his death was sadness about what a waste it had all been.

I went to the funeral home to help Mom and Dad plan the service. They had asked David to join us, but he refused. He did attend the funeral.

I've been asked if I thought Tommy had abused David as he had me. I never saw any indicators of that, and honestly, I'd like to believe if he had, then David might have been more protective of me.

David and Tommy did have a connection that I never shared with them. Although their personalities were at odds, they would occasionally go out and drink together.

The funeral home where Tommy's service was held was doing some work on their sidewalks and parking lot. During visitation they were using a jackhammer. In the front of the room, it wasn't intrusive, but David was holding court with his friends in the back of the room beside a window. I was talking to some people when David walked up and pulled me away.

"YOU need to get them to cut the jackhammering out."

My instinct was to say, "Why don't you?" But I just smiled and said, "I will," and did.

I had hoped that with Tommy's passing, David and I might grow closer. I honestly tried. My parents even asked us both to try.

David told them, "That's up to him."

I eventually gave up.

I tried connecting with David when he had his serious health scare a couple of years before his death. I was rebuffed once again. We spoke very little in the final years of his life.

I've said before that I don't have regrets about not being a cis girl in my childhood. The abuse that Tommy put me through, the strained relationship with David, and the narcissistic behavior of my mother are reasons I am thankful that Stephen existed. If I had been a cis girl, I am convinced these situations would have been much more traumatic.

There is a recurring theme in my childhood. I have no way of knowing if it is related to my trans identity or not. I suspect it is. My parents and siblings always expected me to be the peacemaker, the responsible one, the one that accommodated others' behavior, the one that apologized to end a disagreement, the one that would be expected to help my mother with cooking or cleaning, etc.—at least in those days, those expectations would usually be placed on the female child.

When I turned eighteen, my mother came to me and informed me that I was named the executor of their estate in their will because she knew I'd "do the right thing."

When Tommy passed, she came to me with a plan to sell their house to David and me for one dollar so that in the future, if they ended up with huge medical bills, it wouldn't be lost. I told her that my preference would be to just let David have the house, since he would actually live there and I already owned my own home.

This made her furious—that I was "too good for her house!" I encouraged her many times over the years to make arrangements so he could own the house at their passing. She refused. I honestly believe her intention in including me in the sale was that she knew David would end up living there and I'd ensure it would be taken care of, insurance paid, etc.

The final time this issue was raised was sometime after David had passed and Dad's health had started to decline. She was always concerned that the state or government was going to take what she had worked so hard for in her life. I told her that if she wanted to preserve the house, she could now sell it to me.

She snapped, "You didn't want it when I offered it. You're not getting it now!"

In the final years of her life, as Deanna started to emerge, I became better at setting boundaries with her treatment of me. This did not go over particularly well with her, and she became her most hateful towards me.

I had offered for years for them to move into my house. They always refused.

The final time that Dad went home from a nursing home stay, I was vehemently opposed to it—as was the nursing care facility. It was simply going to be an unsafe situation for both of them. My mother insisted that he come home. Dad was aware it wasn't a good idea and decided they should now move in with me. At that point I wasn't sure I was equipped to handle both of them, but I agreed.

Mom refused and insisted he was coming home. She could adequately care for him. He went home. It was during this time that Dad said to me through tears, "I'm so thankful we haven't lost you. Your brothers would never have been able to do for us what you do. I'm sorry your mother does you the way she does."

It floored me.

I shared what my mother had written about my brothers in Pt. 1:

Tommy: Loving—meeting new people AND learning to use them.

David: Being difficult.

I didn't read her responses until after she passed.

This is what she wrote about me:

Stephen: Loving. Generous. Ambitious.

Again, I was floored.

I'm not convinced she would have meant "ambitious" as a compliment and questioned if her kind words were a result of my having bought the book—this is where my therapist would say, "Stop it."

I choose to believe those were her true feelings.

Understand that my sharing these stories is in no way an attempt to be Christina Crawford and spread salacious rumors about people who can't defend themselves.

If you were fortunate to know and/or love any member of my family, I am very glad. There was much to love about each of them. I don't believe any pain in our relationships was intentional. I don't believe a person gets up in the morning and intends to cause pain that way. They were all products of their environment, just as I or anyone else is.

I loved my family very much.

When you grow up, you accept that your life is the way the world works. Abuse, anger, resentments, etc. do not cancel out good times and genuine love.

In no way do I want to suggest that any issues I dealt with make me somehow better. I have my own challenges. Not a day goes by that I don't catch myself acting or thinking in a way one of my family members might have done; sometimes that is good and sometimes it is not.

I am happy to report that I genuinely think Deanna is better at showing grace than Stephen was. Stephen existed to protect and most often acted accordingly.

I've stated before that I didn't have a fear of sharing my transition with my parents, but the circumstances of their decline prevented me from doing so. My parents nor my brothers ever got to meet Deanna.

That may be sad, but it is also a blessing.

I am fine and in the best place I have ever been in my life.

My protector Stephen absorbed and dealt with so much of the pain from my past.

Deanna doesn't have to live there.

how it feels . . .

January 10, 2025

"How Does It Feel?"

A former student I stay in touch with always concludes our conversations with a question: "How does it feel?"

It's a sweet question—non-specific, simple, and one that I wish more people would ask the trans community.

"How does it feel?"

Sometimes I ask him to clarify—how does what feel?

"How does it feel to change your name?"

It feels uplifting and comforting.

"How does it feel to be addressed as "ma'am?"

It feels amazing and fills me with pride.

"How does it feel to be on HRT?"

It feels like I am alive for the first time.

"How does it feel to wear a bra every day?"

It feels comforting. Nothing is better than a well-fitting bra—except maybe taking it off at the end of the day.

"How does it feel to have an orchiectomy?"

It feels like the best thing that has happened to me.

"How does it feel?"

It feels lucky. I love that my experiences are unique. I get to live my truth.

"How does it feel?"

In a word, it feels right.

It feels right.

out of the mouths . . .

January 13, 2025

I attended a Trans Support Group meeting this past weekend. There were several new folks there, mostly young people.

One new girl—early twenties—was just starting her journey. She and I talked quite a bit.

At the conclusion of our meeting, she came up to me and sweetly asked, "Do you mind if I ask you something?"

I said, "Ask me anything."

She replied, "This may sound weird, but could you be my grandmother?"

I smiled and said, "You BITCH!"

Her eyes widened. "Oh no, what—did I say something wrong?"

"Your *GRANDMOTHER*? Couldn't I just be your cool aunt?"

She answered very seriously, "But I already have an aunt . . ."

Then a realization came across her face. "Oh! You thought I was calling you old! NO, NO! You're just so nice, like what I've always thought a grandmother would be like."

I laughed. "I'm okay with that."

I'm currently looking for an Old Person Support Group . . .

playin' around . . .

January 18, 2025

I've attempted to write about this subject multiple times. Every time I try, I end up getting caught in arguments against the talking points people use to justify their opinions—without addressing what I believe is the real issue.

This week, the U.S. House of Representatives voted to ban trans girls from girls' sports.

At least our trans boys apparently pose no threat to anyone.

In many ways, I feel I don't have much skin in this game. I'm not a trans girl athlete, and I'm almost 100% certain I'll never have a cis or trans daughter who might face this situation. If I did, perhaps my opinion would be different. For example, I'm very much opposed to the death penalty; however, I also recognize that my opinion might change if someone I loved were murdered.

But then comes the question: "Aren't you, as a trans person, just looking to take medals and scholarships away from cis girls, and invade their locker rooms so they feel uncomfortable?"

Ugh.

My honest reaction to sports has always been: "It's just a game!" My interest in sports was limited to two things:

1) Girls' cheerleading uniforms—because I would have loved to wear one.

2) Boys in baseball pants—because . . . DAMN.

I never understood spending hours watching a game on TV—or even the football game my brother got for Christmas one year. My Spin Art made sense to me; tiny plastic football players on a vibrating metal board did not.

Even before I discovered theatre, I was far more interested in the arts. At Christmas, I never got sports equipment or games. Instead, Santa brought me an Etch A Sketch, Spirograph, Creepy Crawlers, Lite-Brite, Monster Maker, Snoopy Snow Cone Maker (culinary arts!), and so on.

I got my first taste of theatre in sixth grade. I had been in 4-H for several years after a brief, predictable stint in Cub Scouts. As if there were ever a choice: camping vs. a Martha White baking contest? (And yes, I won the Martha White baking contest.) As a Cub Scout, I did manage to win a Pinewood Derby trophy—not for speed, but for "Best Design."

In sixth grade, I played the role of "City Slicker" in a 4-H play for June Dairy Month. My character's car broke down near a dairy farm, and the farmer (and the animals) taught me all the wonderful things created because of their work. We even toured the production across Middle Tennessee.

I was a star. I was hooked.

But as I grew older and began to pursue theatre seriously, I faced a harsh reality: in this profession, getting a job often depends on how you look, how old you are, the color of your skin, your gender, and more. No matter how talented I was, I knew I'd face limitations.

Why are you rattling on about theatre in a post about trans girls in sports?

Because there are parallels.

No one banned me from pursuing acting because of who I was or how I looked. I made my own choices. Fortunately, I had a professor who opened another part of theatre to me—design. Did I mention I once painted an award-winning car as a Cub Scout? That talent carried over. I discovered my true passion working backstage, and I found my place.

That's the point I'm laboring to make: there should be nuance, understanding, and yes, grace in this issue.

I've had cis people who are allies say, "The trans community is never going to win on the sports issue."

But finding a place for everyone should never be a win-or-lose situation.

In fact, many cis friends are surprised when I share that most trans people I know agree with the ban on trans girls in sports. I find that both disturbing and deeply disappointing.

The Biden administration initially suggested the issue be handled on a case-by-case basis. I don't think that's an unreasonable place to start.

There is very little in this world that is black and white.

Trans girls are children.

Everyone deserves to feel safe. But my existence—or a child's mere existence—is not a threat to anyone.

All this energy and effort would be far better spent finding a place for everybody.

what a boob . . .

January 31, 2025

A cis friend of mine recently went in for her annual mammogram.

All was good.

When she was telling me about her experience, she suddenly stopped. With guarded curiosity, she asked, "So... will you have to get mammograms?"

"Yes, I will."

Suddenly excited, she said, "Well, I'm going with you for your first one!"

She then launched into detailed descriptions of the different positions I'd have to be in and the various discomforts I'd get to experience. I think she was a little disappointed when I explained that the recommendation is for the first mammogram to take place five years after starting HRT.

I then mentioned that people don't talk about it much, but men can develop breast cancer too. She told me her male cousin is a survivor.

"You'll probably like this too," I added. "When I started hormones, my doctor told me there was a very slight possibility I'd notice some discharge. If I did, I needed to let him know."

She shared that a discharge had actually led to her cousin's diagnosis—it's how many men discover they have breast cancer.

I told her that wasn't exactly what my doctor meant.

When he told me to let him know if I noticed any discharge, I asked, "You mean I could actually...?"

"Yes. It is possible—not likely, but possible."

Apparently, I smiled.

He chuckled and said, "They always smile when I tell them that."

It's true: some trans women can lactate. There are even cases of cis men producing milk. Studies show that it's just as healthy as cis women's milk.

So how does that happen?

Some people mistakenly believe that all embryos start as female. That's not quite true—sex is determined the moment the sperm fertilizes the egg. But if the embryo is male, those characteristics develop later. In the meantime, all embryos begin with the same early characteristics, which we think of as "feminine."

That's why men develop nipples. And those nipples come fully equipped with milk ducts.

We all have much more in common than we like to admit.

Suck on that!

mr. mcbride . . .

February 8, 2025

The other day, the first openly trans representative, Sarah McBride, was recognized on the House floor as "the *gentleman* from Delaware... **Mr.** McBride." Representative McBride ignored the rudeness of the address and proceeded to give her speech as planned.

Ms. McBride was greeted into the House with a ban on where she could use the bathroom. Many argued that she should have fought the ban. I'm sure the same folks will argue she should have taken on the representative who addressed her inappropriately.

I personally believe Ms. McBride made the smart decision in both cases. There are plenty of people who will speak out about these discriminatory and rude acts. If Ms. McBride had spoken out, she would have become the story. She would be further vilified by her detractors. She chose not to fuel their pathetic attempts at attention.

Ms. McBride has the strength to persevere against these childish acts.

The sad part is that the representative who chose to misgender her in such a public forum—clearly in an attempt to make headlines—represents the citizens of her district. Without a doubt, there is a young person in that district questioning who and what they are. That young person is not only terrified by the actions being taken by our government but is also dealing with friends, family, school, and more. This representative chose to make that young person feel even more scared, even more alone.

It is shameful.

We all make choices every day where we can choose kindness and respect over our personal beliefs. That is how a decent person behaves.

I have said so many times—transition is 100% a selfish act. It must be. There is no other way it could happen.

The idea that I, or any other trans person, takes this journey in order to challenge you or your beliefs is beyond idiotic.

I couldn't care less if you choose not to address me by my legal name or my preferred pronouns. That choice says much more about you than it does about me. If your belief system or gender identity is so fragile that you feel compelled to address me as "him" or "sir," then by all means, do so. Your choice will never change who or what I am.

It will, however, potentially hurt those who don't have the advantages or strengths that I am fortunate enough to possess. Those people who can't see a therapist, can't pursue medical care, don't have a support system of friends and family—those are the ones you are hurting. It is incredibly sad if that is what your faith teaches you.

When (or if) you reach your heaven, I doubt very seriously you'll be asked about my sins.

Tell Peter I said, "HAAAAAYYYY..."

February 9, 2025

I've shared before that "passing," or more accurately not being able to "pass," was the main factor in delaying my pursuit of transition.

I realized I was using this measure as an excuse. When I accepted that I would never be passable—and that it really didn't matter—my world changed.

At this point in my journey, I think I am passing. It feels conceited in some ways to state that. Believe me, I'm not suggesting that I'm some great beauty, but I think my being accepted as myself has much to do with my style, my energy, and how I carry myself. The biggest element of passing is that most people simply accept what is presented to them. No one, other than some members of Congress, is actively "looking" for a trans girl.

Passing feels amazing, but it comes with pangs of guilt.

Why guilt?

Because now more than ever, it is vital that people like me are seen. People need to know a trans or nonbinary person. They need to know we are nothing to fear. They need to know we are just trying to live our lives.

I initially thought the goal would be to transition and then become invisible—to move and work someplace where no one would know. But that plan came with the fear that someone would discover my secret. Much of the early reading I did on transition suggested things like: move somewhere new; eliminate all social media; change both first and last names; cut off old relationships; and so on. As brutal as those suggestions sound, that was the norm expected by the gatekeepers of gender care in the recent past.

Last week was a good week in many ways.

I'm embarrassed to admit how much it makes my day when I get an affirming comment or feel like no one suspects I wasn't born Deanna. Highlights included a woman complimenting my perfume and a lady in the checkout line turning around to say, "Oh my god, you are so cute!"

On Thursday, on my way home from work, I stopped at the mall just to walk around.

I ended up buying a new purse. (A Snoopy purse—super cute!)

While paying for it, the young man behind the counter asked if I wanted to join the store's rewards program.

I started to say, "No, I really don't want to get . . ."

He cut me off: "I promise to check all the boxes that'll prevent you from getting annoying daily emails."

I like the store and there was no one behind me waiting, so I said, "Okay."

He asked the expected questions: "Name . . . email . . . phone number; promise no texts . . ."

I shared my phone number.

"Are you from Oklahoma?"

"I use ta live there."

"I grew up in Oklahoma. Primarily Clinton."

"I use ta live in Weatherford."

"What on earth did you do in Weatherford?"

"I use ta teach at Small Town State University."

"Do you still teach?"

"I use ta teach at PRU."

He was finishing filling out the rewards form, smiled, and said, "You seem to have a lot of use tas."

"Oh, I have a couple of big ones." (This wasn't as flirty as it might sound.)

"Really? What's your biggest use ta?"

I have no idea why I said what I said next. It wasn't planned, and it surprised me that it came out. Without missing a beat I said, "I used ta be a boy."

He looked up with a surprised expression and said, "I would have never known that."

I said, "Thank you, that's nice to hear."

"That's really great."

We finished the transaction, and I went on my way.

I have always dreaded the moments where I was put in the position of having to "out" myself. Yet here I purposely did it in a situation where I had no real reason to. I've yet to fully understand why I did it. There are people who would say I was "shoving it in someone's face." Maybe that is the reason. The young man who waited on me did nothing at all other than be kind and respectful. There was absolutely no issue with him.

But there is a big part of me that feels a drive to be seen and heard as the trans person I am—especially in our current environment. So many would prefer that people like me "pass" and stay silent. They would have no issue with my community if we just stayed quiet and accepted whatever they chose to dish out to us.

I cannot begin to explain the empowerment and confidence I have found in my authenticity. This is what scares people about any marginalized group.

I'm not sure what this means for future encounters.

car washer . . .

February 20, 2025

A couple of nice moments today.

I was in Lowe's, and a young man who worked there came up to me and asked, "Ma'am, could I help you with anything?"

I thought about whether anyone in Lowe's had ever said to Stephen, "Sir, could I help you with anything?"

I don't think Stephen ever heard that.

I smiled.

Even though it's freezing, I stopped to run my car through the car wash to get rid of the road ick.

When I pulled up to the kiosk to select and pay, there was an attendant there.

He said, "Which wash would you like today, Ma'am?"

I said, "The middle one."

He pushed the button, and I reached out of the window with my card.

He put his hand up to block my card and said, "Your wash is free today, Ma'am."

I said, "Really?"

"Yes, Ma'am." He pushed some numbers, and the gate went up for entry.

I smiled.

When I shared my day with my friend (she is cis, by the way), she said, "You do realize we are under attack?"

I do.

I also don't run to post on Facebook every time someone calls me "ma'am."

I can—and do—get angry, scared, ready to fight, etc.

What I will not do is sacrifice my joy.

The biggest reward of living authentically is finding such amazing joy. I will not surrender it to the horror show we are living.

This is not a "trans thing." You will find great strength in discovering yours every day. I highly recommend it.

softer . . .

February 23, 2025

The most amazing thing about being trans for me is experiencing a duality in my life. I have successfully presented as both male and female, and I am grateful to have lived both on some level. I've always been fascinated by how differently I am treated in each role.

I have been fortunate that all the important people in my life have been supportive of my transition.

I have always had more female friends than male—perhaps that is indicative of my being trans. Both my female and male friends were generous from the start of my journey, but I think, in general, women are more at ease with it. I only say this because women are much more curious and comfortable asking questions. I imagine men with trans male friends don't ask them many questions either.

I never told my closest male friend that I was transitioning. His wife was the first "civilian" I told. After my conversation with her, she asked if I wanted her to tell him or if I'd rather do it myself. I knew it wouldn't be a problem for him, but I thought he might need some time to process it. I'm not sure it was the right decision, but I asked her to tell him. As I expected, he was—and is—very supportive.

He is like a brother to me. Our relationship is what I would have liked to have with my actual brothers as adults. I thoroughly enjoy giving him a hard time and aggravating him. I've often said to him that I was "the annoying little brother you never wanted."

In my first year of HRT, I spent the majority of my time presenting in an androgynous state, but whenever I visited them, I got to go full fem. At first, I worried that things might be awkward for both of us as I navigated being myself. I was concerned that my appearance might embarrass him. I asked him to tell me if I ever wore something or looked some way that would make him uncomfortable being seen with me.

He never did.

There have been many sweet and funny moments between us since I started transitioning.

The first time I wore a bathing suit in front of him, I said, "Stop looking at my chest!"

He then looked at my chest and asked, "Are those real?"

He laughed when I was proud to show off my first tan line on my boobs.

When he sees me do something feminine—like refresh my lipstick, put lotion on my hands, or wear my hair in a turbie twist after washing—he shakes his head and says, "I'm glad I'm not a girl."

Early in my transition, when I was nowhere near passing, he wanted to go to a sports bar to watch a football game but didn't want to go alone. I told him I'd go with him, and if he wanted, I'd dress as a boy. He said, "I would NEVER want you to do that."

Last summer I asked him if he was okay with me and my new self.

He said, "Of course I am . . . but you are different."

I was surprised by his comment and said, "I'm the same person."

"You are . . . but it's different."

"How so?"

"I don't know, you're just . . . softer."

"What does that mean?"

"You're just softer. Look, it's not bad—it's just different."

After a pause he continued, "It's just . . . Stephen was one of my few male friends. He's not here now, and it's an adjustment for me."

It's true—he does have a lot of women in his life.

As a trans person, I had years to think about how Stephen wasn't my true self. Trans folks are often so happy and euphoric about shedding our false selves that we don't always recognize or appreciate that the "person" we shed was someone's cherished family member or friend. Family and friends often need a mourning period as they let go of someone they cared about for so long.

I just looked at him and said, "I'm sorry."

"No. Don't be sorry—why would you be sorry?"

With tears forming in my eyes, I said, "I've always said I was the little brother you never wanted . . . now I guess I'm the sister you don't need."

He smiled and said, "Yeah . . . but you're my favorite sister."

I cried.

He has never said anything, but I know he hates how much—and how easily—I cry now.

I suppose my tears are a sign of being "softer," but I'm happy to have them as a new way to aggravate him.

rebirth . . .

March 2, 2025

What follows is an email I sent to both my state senator and state representative on Thursday February 20, 2025:

Dear Representative XXXXXXX:

My name is Deanna J. Haynes. I currently live in Henry County, Tennessee, and was born in Maury County, Tennessee.

On March 4, 2024, my name was legally changed from Stephen E. Haynes to Deanna J. Haynes by the Hon. XXXXXX XXXXXXXX, chancellor for the XXth Judicial District Chancery Court of Tennessee.

Judge XXXXXXX instructed me to immediately update my driver's license, my social security card, and my birth certificate. My social security card and my driver's license were updated with my new name within hours of my court appearance. The office of vital records required that my request for an updated birth certificate be handled by mail. I mailed all the requested documents, including my original birth certificate and payment for the service.

The first week of April 2024 I received a form letter from their office notifying me that they had received all my paperwork. I was advised to check their website for the expected arrival of my new document. The letter stated the website would be regularly updated to reflect accurate wait times. The form letter further stated that if I didn't receive my new document within that time frame to contact their office so they could "investigate." The website indicated a wait time of eight (8) months. I checked the website monthly to see if the time frame had changed. It remained eight (8) months for the rest of the year.

In early December 2024, nine months after sending in my request I contacted their office via the website to inquire about my document. I received a form letter email stating they had received my request and opened a "ticket."

In early January I submitted another request asking for an update on when to expect my document.

The following week I called their office and was asked to leave a message. Their voice mail message stated that I would receive a call back within three (3) to four (4) weeks. I have received no return call.

Late January I received an email informing me that my two previous email inquiries had been combined into one "ticket." No other information was given.

This morning, I once again checked the website for wait times. It indicates that it was updated on "2/14/2025" and now offers a wait time of "12 months . . . for court orders received prior to July 1, 2024."

I am approximately two (2) weeks aways from my one-year anniversary of legally changing my name.

I need my birth certificate.

I would sincerely appreciate any direction or help you might give in making this happen.

With all due respect,

Deanna J. Haynes

I was shocked when I received a response from both the senator's and the representative's offices within an hour of sending my email. Both responses came from legislative assistants, and both said they would pass my letter on to the Office of Vital Records.

I was struck by the salutations used in each letter. The senator's office response began with a simple, pleasant "Good Afternoon," while the representative's note opened with "Hello Ms. Haynes."

I was glad they had responded and offered to forward my note. I didn't expect to hear anything further from either of them.

On Wednesday, February 26, I received another email from the representative's assistant. After the salutation, "Hello Deanna!" I was asked to "see" the attached emails. They included a short exchange between the assistant and the legislative liaison in the Department of Health. In the first email, dated Thursday, February 20, the liaison said he would take care of it. In the second, he shared that the new document had been mailed on Monday, February 24.

The document arrived in my mailbox on Thursday, February 27—just one week after I sent my email. It had been processed on Friday, February 21, only one day after my message.

I have heard nothing further from the senator's office.

I feel lucky.

I am VERY grateful to the assistant in the representative's office. She was professional, prompt, helpful, respectful, and simply a nice person doing her job. I have not shared the representative's name because I am not a fan, and I doubt that if he had personally answered his emails, I would have received the same response or result.

It's easy to imagine that any trans person requesting an updated birth certificate might have their request set aside. Who knows if that is the case, as there are many reasons someone might need to update their name on a document. I don't believe people like me make up the majority of requests.

I don't mind waiting my turn. If you say it will take eight months, I accept that. But if it's going to take longer, the least you can do is notify the requester and offer a reason. I wonder how many requests for name changes on birth certificates were stacked above and below mine.

Within hours of my name change, I had a new "temporary" driver's license and "temporary" Social Security card. I received both permanent documents within two weeks.

It took four weeks to get my updated passport (yes, before the return of the orange menace).

It took almost a year to finally obtain my new birth certificate. That should not be acceptable for any citizen of this state.

I had been told to expect my former name to be "**X**'d" out, with my new name typed above it. I don't know when they stopped that ridiculous practice. Tennessee still does not allow gender marker changes.

With all that is going on in the world, I know this was a minor inconvenience. Still, I'm putting it in my "win" column.

The reply from the assistant was another reminder of how surprising it feels when someone treats me with kindness and respect. One of the biggest changes I've noticed since beginning my journey is the constant question in my mind: "I wonder if they're going to be nice to me?" My entire life, while enjoying "cis" white male privilege, I never once thought about that before engaging with someone.

happy . . .

March 4, 2025

Happy Birthday . . . Happy Anniversary . . . Happy Born Again . . .

I'm not sure what the right phrase is for today, as it marks one year of my being legally Deanna Jean. What an amazing year it has been.

A friend commented, "Wow, I can't believe it's already been a year. It doesn't seem like it's been that long, does it?"

For me, it feels longer. It feels so natural—like this is the way it has always been.

I never realized I could be this happy and content in my life.

Thank you to everyone who has supported me in being me.

This week is Nurse Week at work, and I get to celebrate as BTMC's newest (pretend) nurse—

Nurse Haynes.

So much joy!

5 ... 10 ... 40 ...

March 7, 2025

Five days. Ten medical students. Forty hours of medical simulation. An amazing week.

Yep—here she goes again, spouting off about how amazing everything is for her. Okay, maybe not everything ... but wow—what a week I've had.

Some highlights ...

The sims went off more or less without a hitch. Out of the ten students on my case, most of them got the treatment right. But what really struck me were the ones who got something else right. In addition to working through the medicine, four of the students showed true humanity and compassion. To see young men and women under tremendous pressure, in a stressful situation, take the time to reach out and hold the hand of their "patient" ... it was beautiful.

Since starting this job, I've made some friends. This week, I became close with several people. The whole experience reminded me of tech week in theatre: we were tired; little aggravations popped up; we laughed, worked hard, and had each other's backs. I'm not exaggerating when I say it felt like that. Three people asked me very respectful questions about being trans. A few others, who I hadn't gotten to spend much time with, asked me to sit with them next time so we could get to know each other better. Honestly, I almost felt like the belle of the ball.

And then—there was a brief, amazing conversation with a very handsome ER doctor. (At least 6'4" . . . swoon!) He came in one day as a faculty observer while the students were working. I noticed him immediately—and noticed him glancing my way—but we didn't interact during the sim. Later, as I was heading to the parking garage, I found myself walking beside him. He started talking, and if anyone had overheard us, they would have assumed we were old friends. It was only twelve to fifteen minutes, but it was such a bright, human connection.

"So, what kind of nurse are you?"

"The fake kind."

"Seriously?"

"Seriously."

We talked a bit about what I do, and he shared that he wasn't exactly sure why he picked emergency medicine. Our conversation ended when he had to turn toward the Emergency Department.

As he walked away, I called out, "Hey!"

He stopped and turned.

"Go save some lives!"

He smiled, said, "You know it, girl," winked, and walked away.

There's little chance our paths will cross again, but he truly made my day. I hope I made his.

I also worked with two amazing women this week.

The first was a retired heart surgery nurse—kind, patient, and generous in teaching me the ropes. She told me many stories of being called in the middle of the night to "crack open a chest."

The second woman played "the patient." She made me cry more than once with the things she said. We'd worked together before and always had nice conversations. But this week, she shared something personal: she has a trans nephew, and she wished the world understood how special trans people are. She told me the example our community sets—the courage to be yourself and to choose happiness—is something that should be celebrated by everyone.

She also confessed that she had hurt her nephew many times by accidentally misgendering him. Though he always forgave her, she worried there would come a day when he wouldn't.

I told her that for some of us, misgendering can be deeply painful—and that many in our community really struggle with it. For me, I don't let it bother me unless I'm certain someone is doing it on purpose.

She looked at me and said, "I knew that's how you felt, and it's part of what makes you such a special girl."

I asked what she meant.

She said, "One of the times we were on the same case, I accidentally referred to you with the wrong gender. You didn't say anything, but I could see on your face that you'd heard it. I was convinced you wouldn't want to talk to me anymore. I felt sick to my stomach that I'd hurt you. But then you just kept talking like nothing had happened. That's when I knew—you are so special."

sweet ? . . .

March 25, 2025

The days I work, I usually arrive at least an hour early. This helps me avoid traffic and gives me time to review my notes. There's a café in the courtyard at the base of our building, and I usually stop there to get a beverage—and sometimes a cookie—while I go over the case.

There's an assistant manager there most days. She's sweet and works her tail off, even though people are often rude about having to wait. I always try to be nice to her, and she's told me before how much she appreciates it.

This morning, while I was waiting in line, she just walked off when it was my turn. A moment later she came back with a Diet Coke and a cookie, handed them to me, and said, "It's on the house today, sweet girl."

I said, "You don't need to do that."

She smiled and said, "I do, because you are the sweetest person I see all day."

It's official: Deanna is much nicer than Stephen ever was.

HRT X 2 . . .

March 27, 2025

Two years ago, I was officially diagnosed with gender dysphoria and began HRT.

I was thrilled, scared, excited, apprehensive—you name it.

I honestly wish I had a video of the appointment I had with my doctor that day. I was so nervous, quiet, and uncomfortable as I answered the questions required for consent. I was not Deanna that day—in name or in many other ways. I was still legally Stephen and was using the name Bethany. I was very much still in the protective cocoon I had built over the years.

When I met Dr. Estra, my first thought was that he looked like a teenager. My comment about his youthful appearance should in no way suggest a lack of confidence in his abilities or skills, but rather a nod to my own feeling like a total antiquity. He was extremely professional and kind to me. He showed no surprise or judgment at my answers. He thoroughly reviewed the "what to expect" checklist and the risks to my health that hormone therapy might impose.

I consented to treatment that day. It is, without a doubt, the best decision I have ever made.

I saw him regularly over the next several months as he monitored and adjusted my treatment. One hormone patch, then a testosterone blocker, then a second patch, then progesterone—all stepped in as my levels were assessed.

Last year I had my one-year check-in, and it was a memorable appointment for me.

He had a fellow working with him that day, and she participated in the appointment. We hit it off immediately. I was wearing my gummy bear necklace and earrings, and she complimented them. That led to a discussion of the awesomeness of TJ Maxx. She mentioned retail therapy, and I added that the real therapy was long bubble baths. She sighed and said she wished she had time for one.

You get the idea.

I remember glancing at Dr. Estra and seeing him grinning as the fellow and I chatted. I'll never know what he was thinking, but I've imagined it was something like: 1) This really is just two girls talking, and 2) Seriously, I have other patients waiting!

It's no secret that trans people have immense affection for their gender-affirming care providers. In a state like Tennessee, there are so few that many patients sit on waiting lists. I am so grateful for the professionals who do this work. It is no overstatement when I say: I am very lucky.

The moment that stands out most from that one-year appointment was when my doctor first walked into the exam room. His mouth literally dropped. He had seen me several times over the course of the year, but this was the first time since I had fully socially transitioned. I was legally Deanna, and I felt euphoric.

He smiled broadly and said, "I was going to ask how you're doing, but my God, Deanna, you are absolutely glowing."

I was. I still am.

epilogue . . .

March 29, 2025

I was in Paris (TN) today to do yard work at the "country house." Fortunately, I finished before the rain started. For dinner, I decided to treat myself to a cheeseburger from Culver's (yummy!).

On the way home, I decided to stop at Marshalls and Bealls—because, of course, I did.

Not needing anything, I naturally found a really cute purse at Marshalls. An incredibly sweet young man waited on me at the counter.

He picked up the purse and said, "This is a really cool purse."

I agreed.

When he shared the total, he started his speech to get me to sign up for a store credit card. Before he got too far into it, I whipped out my TJ MAXX/MARSHALLS/AT HOME credit card.

He smiled and said, "I knew you were a smart lady."

He placed my purse in a bag, then pulled it back out and said, "I'm going to take the paper out of this so you don't have to deal with it at home."

He should really wait tables so he could earn tips.

I then walked to Bealls.

Right inside the door, two kids were sitting on a bench next to a table of hand-bags—obviously an older brother and younger sister who looked to be around eight or nine. I had just bought a purse at Marshalls, so naturally, I needed to look at more.

When I started browsing the table, the kids began whispering and giggling. I glanced over and caught them looking at me a couple of times. I didn't say anything, but it was clear they were talking about me. It deflated me, and my feelings took a bruising.

I moved down the aisle of bags. About halfway down, I noticed the young girl had gotten up and started down the same aisle—pretending to look at purses but still eyeing me.

She moved closer.

I finally said, "Sweetie, did you need something?"

She said, "I'm sorry, I was just trying to see your shirt."

"OHHHHHH." A huge smile spread across my face.

"It's my favorite movie."

I was wearing a *Wicked* shirt. (A similar situation happened last summer involving my "Mouseketeer" shirt and a leering pharmacist.)

I said, "Elphaba is my favorite."

"Mine too!"

"She's beautiful, isn't she?"

"Yes, she is!"

Her mother then called for her, and she said, "See you later," before running off.

I so wish I had a *Wicked* shirt I could have given her.

I am ashamed that I immediately assumed something negative, but I'm grateful this child reminded me of such an important lesson about assumptions.

I turned the corner and found an amazing gummy bear wallet.

A fantastic day.

acknowledgments . . .

amazing beautiful people . . .

John Caterina, Nancy Caterina, Audrey Hamilton,

Myra Carlock, Steve Strickler, Jackson Garner, Christine Woodworth,

Laura Skaug, Myna Sowell, Chris Bosen

A very special thanks to "Dr. Estra," "Dr. Surge," my therapist and all the medical professionals that have provided such excellent care for me. I will never be able to fully express my gratitude for all you do for me and so many others in what is often a hostile world.

about the author . . .

Deanna Haynes holds the Master of Fine Arts degree in Theatrical Design &
Technology from Louisiana State University. She has worked for over twenty
years as a Professor of Theatre and Speech. Deanna has provided designs for over
eighty theatrical productions throughout her career and has worked in most every
area of theatre. She currently works as a standardized patient in Nashville, TN.
She is pursuing becoming a certified Life Transition Coach serving the LGBTQ+
community. She lives in Middle Tennessee with the best boy in the world, a black
lab mix named Poncho. This is her first book.

Please visit www.AuntJoansCabin.net

www.ingramcontent.com/pod-product-compliance
Lightning Source LLC
Chambersburg PA
CBHW070913130626
46555CB00001B/116